GETTING STARTED
knitting

GETTING STARTED

knitting

Jennifer **Worick**

IP INTERWEAVE PRESS

Editor: Ann Budd
Technical Editor: Jean Lampe
Design: Paulette Livers
Production: Pauline Brown
Photo Styling: Ann Swanson
Photography: Joe Coca
Illustration: Sara Boore
Proofreader and Indexer: Nancy Arndt

INTERWEAVE PRESS

201 East Fourth Street
Loveland, Colorado 80537 USA
www.interweave.com

Printed in China through Asia Pacific Offset

Library of Congress Cataloging-in-Publication Data
Worick, Jennifer.
  Getting started knitting / Jennifer Worick, author.
    p. cm.
  Includes index.
  ISBN 1-931499-94-2
  1. Knitting. 2. Knitting--Patterns. I. Title.
TT820.W69 2006
746.43'2--dc22
                                        2005020186

10 9 8 7 6 5 4 3 2 1

acknowledgments

This book would not be possible without the design talents of Courtney Kelley, Lisa R. Myers, and Grace Anna Robbins, who provided the many patterns in this book. Their skill in creating deceptively simple projects continues to floor me. Thanks also to Dorlynn Starn for her help in knitting up projects lickety-split.

The Interweave staff—particularly Rebecca Campbell, Ann Budd, Betsy Armstrong, and Linda Stark—are a perfect blend of professional and patient, and I'm forever grateful for their collaboration and care. Thanks also to Jean Lampe, Jaime Guthals, Joe Coca, Ann Swanson, Sara Boore, Paulette Livers, and Pauline Brown for bringing their creative talents to the book process.

The projects in this book could never have been created without the yummy yarns supplied by generous manufacturers across the continent. Narrowing down and choosing yarns for each project was both difficult and enjoyable because of the incredible breadth of color and texture available from these companies. Thank you so much for continuing to give knitters new fiber options to play with.

I also have to give a shout out to Jennifer Hill of Hilltop Yarn West in Seattle for supplying some of the yarns photographed in this book. Finally, my deepest thanks to the countless knitters who have aided me in my own journey into the heart of the knitting beast, I mean, adventure. I hope that I can pass on the same level of support and patience they offered me.

contents

Welcome to the Wide World of Knitting!

Knitting seems to be everywhere, and you've finally decided to get in on the action and join in the fun. After seeing one cute knitted item after another, you've decided, "Hey, I'm smart, I'm cute, and I want to make cute things for my cute self—I can do this!" You're right, you can! All it takes is a bit of moxie, yarn, and a pair of needles. Really, that's all!

So let's get to what you really want to know: How and where do you begin? Right here, right now, with this book.

Many books and magazines in the market still seem to be written in Greek, with strange symbols, drawings, and abbreviations. Not this book! Nope, this little gem is what you've been searching for. Not only is it written in plain English, but it will be your tour guide through the wide world of knitting. And your journey will be filled with minimal pain and maximum delight. We'll save the cryptic symbols for later.

Let's get started knitting!

1

The Yarn Store: Needles and Patterns and Yarn, Oh My!

Before we begin our adventure at the yarn shop, here are a few questions to measure your knowledge of the knitting world (and your sense of humor).

A yarn swift is a:

a) knitter with lightning-fast fingers.

b) machine that is used to wind yarn into balls.

c) bird indigenous to the Faroe Islands.

d) technique that involves knitting with only one needle.

Cashmere comes from:

a) heaven. Something this soft couldn't possibly be found on Earth.

b) Turkish sheep raised on a diet of lentils and extra-virgin olive oil.

c) a mill in India now owned by Ralph Lauren.

d) the soft wool of a Himalayan goat.

It is a good idea to knit:

a) during a long flight.

b) in a car that makes frequent and sudden stops.

c) in the bathtub.

d) in a darkened movie theater.

The question a stranger will most likely ask you when he happens upon you knitting:

a) "What are you making?"

b) "How long have you been knitting?"

c) "Is it hard to knit?"

d) "Could you be any cooler?"

To knit a garment, you need:

a) yarn.

b) needles.

c) patience.

d) all of the above.

While it doesn't matter if you know the answers to the first four questions (b, d, a, any letter, respectively), the last question speaks more to the task at hand, namely your first trip to the yarn shop.

Walking into a yarn shop should be pure delight, not anxiety inducing in any way. The staff will be gentle, I promise. In fact, they are by and large enormously knowledgeable, helpful, and eager to walk you through the basic steps in planning a project and buying the appropriate materials. Being armed with a little knowledge and a plan (that you've developed with the help of, ahem, this trusty little book) will help you and your new best friends at the yarn shop make quick and easy decisions.

Most knitters learn to knit by making a scarf, which makes a lot of sense. You are dealing with short rows, you have time to get comfortable working two needles and a ball of yarn (Don't worry if you feel like you have two flippers instead of hands when you are first learning. It's normal.), and you can see immediate results. The rush of seeing fabric actually growing off your needles is one of life's simple pleasures. (This holds true for knitters and non-knitters alike. Once you are knitting up a storm on planes, trains, and automobiles, strangers of every kind will ask what you are making. Knitting is seen as both mystery and miracle to non-knitters.)

You know you want to make a scarf, that much you can tell the salesperson. But what do you need to make it? You may not require a pattern for your first scarf project, but you do need an idea of what you want it to look like.

For instance:
- Do you want it long and skinny or short and wide?
- What color do you want it to be—your favorite jewel tone or a neutral that will go with everything?

THE FIRST PROJECT
Most people knit a scarf for their first project.

Visualize Your Dream Scarf

🖎 Do you want a trendy scarf knit with Muppet-like yarn or one that will stand the test of time?

🖎 Do you want a summer-weight or dead-of-winter-weight scarf?

🖎 Is there a fiber you really like or one that always makes you itch, sneeze, cry, or some combination of the three?

Some of these questions will only be answered after you peruse the yarn offerings. More than one person has entered a yarn shop with the idea in her mind of what she wants to knit, only to find a delicious yarn she can't bear to leave behind or conversely, that the yarn in her mind's eye doesn't exactly exist. Be flexible.

But be wary. The bins and cubbyholes in the yarn shop are going to be chock full of scrumptious yarns. Resist the urge to go hog wild! Keep to the task at hand, namely choosing a yarn for your scarf and then buying enough yarn to complete it. That luscious oatmeal-colored alpaca yarn will still be there when you're ready for your next project. (Just in case, it's not a bad idea to jot down the yarn manufacturer, yarn name, color, and any other pertinent information from the yarn's label.)

A TOUR OF THE YARN SHOP

So that brings us to the main event: shopping! **Yarn stores** can be found virtually anywhere: in basements, storefronts, strip malls, cyberspace. . . . Yarn doesn't have to take up much room so yarn shops can be tucked away off the beaten path. Use the Internet or the Yellow Pages to find a shop close to you and check it out. Weekends and lunch hours, especially in the fall, are often hectic times in the store. Call and find out if the shop offers classes or a weekly knitting circle (knitting circles are excellent opportunities to meet fellow knitters, share ideas, and be inspired by the varied projects). Since space is often at a premium, it may be hard for you to peruse the shop's wares if it's full of avid knitters. For your first trip to the shop, better to go during off hours when you can mull over two shades of mohair or ask the shop owner for assistance.

Okay, what's in the store? First and foremost, yarn! Yarn of every natural and manmade fiber and in every color imaginable will be sorted and placed in bins or cubbyholes. Sometimes **hanks** of yarn are displayed on horizontal rods.

Yarns are commonly sorted by the manufacturer and brand name (for instance, Plymouth Encore—Plymouth produces various yarns and Encore is one of them) or by color. You might find one company's line of cashmere in a bin. It will be identical in **weight** (thickness of yarn strand), **fiber content** (what the yarn is made with), amount of yarn, and **texture** (smooth, fuzzy, a loopy bouclé, etc.), but will vary in color. So if you know you want a thin cashmere yarn but don't know what color you fancy, look for the yarn fiber and weight first and see what colors it comes in second. You may know that you want to knit in a certain shade of pale lemon yellow so look through all the bins and pull out the yellows that you like. Then feel the yarn (rub it against the inside of your wrist if you want to check its scratchiness factor), check the price, and see which one fits your needs and your wallet.

A sale bin will most likely beckon from some cozy corner of the shop. Rifle through the selection and if you find yarn you adore, snap it up. Just make sure to buy enough to complete your project (a pattern will give you specific information on yardage, but you can also ask a salesperson to help you estimate). Check the **dye lot** (a number printed on the label that indicates in which batch of yarn the skein was dyed) to make sure that your yarns will match in color when you are knitting with more than one skein.

There will be a revolving rack, bookshelf, binders, or other displays of patterns, books, and knitting magazines. While you don't need them to knit a scarf, books and magazines are fab ways to learn more about the knitting community and to get your creative juices flowing.

The Yarn Store

Yarn Swift

In a corner of the shop, you might notice an accordion-fold contraption that, if made from wood, looks like it belongs in an Amish farmhouse. It's a **yarn swift,** and it helps you wind the yarn into a workable ball. Just fit a **hank** of yarn over the frame, attach one end of the yarn to a **ball winder,** and turn the handle to wind the yarn into a **ball or skein.** You *do* need to do this (sometimes the yarn shop will do this for you) for yarns that come in hanks. Working with a hank will usually result in a big tangle of yarn, and it's not practical if you want to take your knitting on the road. Your other option is to manually wind the yarn into a ball, which is time-consuming when you just want to be knitting. But it can also be a meditative Zen pursuit if you have the time.

Needles will be displayed on a circular rack or perhaps behind the counter. There are loads of different needle types—straight, circular, double-pointed, cable, tapestry—not to mention sizes. For your purposes, you'll want a set of straight needles. (You can use circular needles and just treat them as straight needles, knitting back and forth along a row. However, it is better to learn the basics with the basics—i.e., straight needles, since it can be tricky to use circular needles at first.) Straight needles are made of wood, bamboo, plastic, or metal, although occasionally you'll find some made from more unusual materials. Metal and plastic needles offer more slip, whereas stitches don't slip quite as easily off wooden or bamboo needles. Any straight needles are fine for your purposes.

Ball Winder

NEEDLES: SIZE DOES MATTER

A general rule of thumb: pair heavier, bulkier yarns with larger (i.e., fatter) needles and thinner or lighter-weight yarns with smaller (or skinnier) needles.

Needles come in lots of different thicknesses. A general rule of thumb is to pair heavier, bulkier yarns with larger (i.e., fatter) needles and thinner or lighter-weight yarns with smaller (or skinnier) needles. Knitting with fine yarn on larger needles will produce lacier, open, loose fabric and knitting with über-bulky yarn on smaller needles will create fabric that's dense and rigid like a sturdy rug or thick tapestry.

The Skinny on Needles

A. *Straight needles:* Used to produce flat knitting, such as a scarf, shawl, or the panel of a sweater, straight needles are usually made of wood, metal, plastic, or bamboo.

B. *Circular needles:* Circular needles are short needles that are attached to each other by nylon cord and are used when "knitting in the round," seamless tubular knitting you might need for a hat, leg warmer, or body of a sweater. Circular needles come in a variety of lengths and can also be used in place of straight needles, especially if you are knitting a large piece of flat knitting, such as a shawl.

C. *Double-pointed needles:* Double-pointed needles (or DPNs) are pointed on both ends like their name suggests. They produce seamless round knitting for small projects such as socks, baby hats, or the crown of a hat.

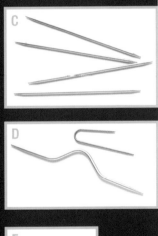

D. *Cable needle:* This is a short, double-pointed needle that is used for creating cables in your knitted work.

E. *Tapestry needle:* While not used for knitting, tapestry needles are an essential part of any knitter's "toolbox." They are used to weave in yarn ends and strands into your garment so they are hidden from view.

Tip: Inventory your needles. If you keep a log of your needle collection, you'll avoid purchasing duplicate needles in the heat of the moment when you are buying materials for a pattern you just picked up at the yarn shop. It doesn't need to be anything fancy. You can maintain an Excel spreadsheet or you can simply jot your needle sizes down under headings of "straight needles," "circular needles" (don't forget to record the length of your circular needles as well), and "double-pointed needles."

Needle Size Conversions

U.S.		Metric	English
0	●	2 mm	14
1	●	2.25 mm	13
2	●	2.75 mm	12
3	●	3.25 mm	11
4	●	3.5 mm	10
5	●	3.75 mm	9
6	●	4 mm	8
7	●	4.5 mm	7
8	●	5 mm	6
9	●	5.5 mm	5
10	●	6 mm	4
10½	●	6.5 mm	2
11	●	8 mm	1
13	●	9 mm	00
15	●	10 mm	0000

The size of a needle might be denoted in several ways, the most common being U.S. and metric sizes (some needles list the English equivalent). A 5.5 mm needle is a U.S. size 9, a nice mid-size needle. Some needles don't list the size on them at all (or the size has been worn away), so it's helpful to have a **needle size guide.** You can buy a metal or plastic needle and knitting gauge ruler, and some books even include them. Before you can even check the **gauge** (the number of knitted stitches in an inch) of your knitting, you need to pick a needle you think will give you the size and effect you're looking to achieve. First look at what yarn and needle size the pattern calls for. If you are knitting with the suggested yarn, start by knitting a **swatch** (a sample square in the suggested stitch pattern) with the recommended needles. You may knit tighter or looser than the pattern designer intended so don't assume that you can start knitting the pattern without checking that you're on target with your gauge. If you are knitting more stitches to the inch than the recommended gauge, try swatching your work on larger needles. If you knit fewer stitches to the inch, reduce your needle size until you find the size that gives you a spot-on gauge.

If you are knitting your first scarf, gauge is not as important, since you are just knitting it to wrap around your neck. Look for a mid-weight yarn, such as a worsted-weight yarn (see chart on page 14), and pair it with needles in the U.S. size 7 to 10 range. Check the yarn label to see what needle size is recommended for the yarn you've selected. (Huge needles are not recommended when learning to knit—your hands, not fingers, end up holding them—and small needles result in dense knitting or a project that takes forever to finish.)

MATERIALS FOR YOUR FIRST PROJECT

You really don't need a truckload of supplies.

Needles and yarn. That's pretty much all you'll need, along with a sense of what you want to knit. As you start knitting, you will be tempted to buy a knitting bag, a needle organizer, straight needles, circular needles, cable needles, tape measure, stitch holders, stitch markers, row counters, big-eye needles, point protectors, books, magazines, patterns, yarn, yarn, yarn.

A kid in a candy store has nothing on a knitter in a yarn store, so think carefully before you buy. You really don't need a truckload of supplies, especially when you're Getting Started, so hold onto your credit card. . . .

To knit a scarf, you will need a pair of needles, some yarn, and later, a tapestry needle to weave the ends of the yarn into your work of art. How much yarn do you need? What size needles should you use? Most yarns feature a paper label that lists a recommended needle size to achieve a certain stitch size, or gauge. While it's not critical to check gauge when making a scarf, it is helpful to have a general idea of what your gauge is when you are figuring out how wide you want your scarf to be.

Just because a **skein** of yarn costs a small fortune, don't despair. You may not need very many skeins (in fact, you may only need one) to knit a scarf, whereas another yarn might come in smaller yardage balls that require that you buy several to make a garment.

Buy more yarn than you need. It's better to have half a ball of yarn left over than to try to find another ball from the same **dye lot** (the skeins of yarn that were all dyed in the same batch). That extra yarn can be used to create fringe or tassels or to edge another garment down the road.

Take your time when picking your yarn. After all, you're going to be spending a *lot* of time with it. For your first project, choose a yarn in a light- to medium-range color. Steer clear of black; stitches will be harder to see. The yarn weight should be on the heavier side. Coupled with big needles, you'll make progress fast, which is extremely gratifying. And not that it matters, of course, but your friends will be wowed by your knitting prowess.

Buy more yarn than you need. It's better to have half a ball of yarn left over than to try to find another ball from the same dye lot.

Tip: Swatches are not only useful when figuring out gauge. Add them to your yarn journal with notes about how the yarn was to knit with. Even check out the yarn's washability before committing your project to the washing machine.

FIGURING OUT YOUR YARN AMOUNT

Tip: If your yarn feels stiff, secure the hank in four places to prevent tangles, and wash the hank in cold water before knitting with it. It'll be a much more pleasing garment to knit and to wear.

Check out the different scarf projects in Chapter 2 (see pages 32–40). Each project lists a recommended yarn, along with the amount of yarn you'll need to complete the project. If you are ever unsure of how much you'll need, err on the side of having too much. You can always add the leftovers to your stash to edge, embellish, or knit a small project later on.

Skeins and balls come in a variety of yardages. Some skeins include so much yarn that you only need one to knit up a shawl or even a sweater, so always check the yarn label against the yardage detailed in the pattern. If you are working without a pattern, buy more than you think you'll need or ask the yarn shop if they'd be so kind as to hold a skein in the same dye lot for you (some yarn shops will even let you return unused yarn, as long as you didn't wind it into a ball).

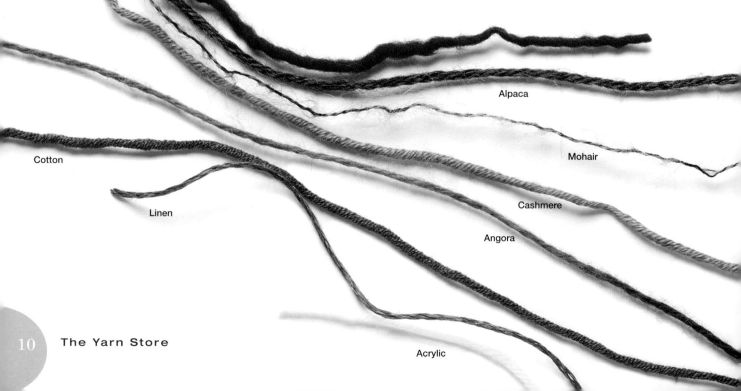

Wool

Alpaca

Cotton

Mohair

Linen

Cashmere

Angora

Acrylic

Fiber Facts

Yarn is made up of all sorts of fibers, both natural and manmade. Some intrepid knitters even manage to knit with dog hair!

Wool: Wool is the most common fiber to knit with. Sheared from sheep, wool is very durable and water-resistant but can be scratchy. Merino wool is the exception; it's soft and a good choice if the garment is going to be worn against the skin and your budget doesn't allow for cashmere. Handwashing is usually recommended for wool, but there are some machine-washable yarns on the market.

Alpaca: Super warm and super soft, alpaca yarn (which comes from—no surprise here—the alpaca) usually comes in earthy, natural tones and, like cashmere, is considered a luxury fiber. Handwashing is recommended.

Mohair: Fuzzy and sometimes itchy, mohair (which comes from a goat) looks great with open, large-gauge projects that aren't worn against the skin. The yarn's long fibers can sometimes shed on you or furniture. Handwash your mohair garments.

Cashmere: The Rolls Royce of yarns, cashmere is buttery soft, comes in a variety of thicknesses and colors, and is taken from the underbelly of the Cashmere goat. Of course, it's pricey, but many would say this yummy fiber is worth every penny. Handwash unless the label indicates otherwise.

Angora: Comes from bunnies. Fuzzy and fine, great to the touch but can shed and sometimes irritate contact-lens wearers. Or maybe that's just me . . . Definitely don't throw this delicate yarn into the washing machine.

Cotton: Absorbent, durable, and machine washable, cotton is great for baby garments and summer projects. It's not a very "fluffy" or flexible yarn, so it can show uneven knitting.

Linen: Linen comes from the flax plant, and like many linen garments that you have in your closet, it is a cool and breathable fiber, a bit stiff, and prone to wrinkling. It's super strong, however, and often machine-washable. And with each washing, a linen garment becomes softer and even more pleasurable to wear (which is hard to imagine, I know).

Acrylic/Polyester: Don't poo-poo these inexpensive, synthetic fibers. They are often machine-washable and dryable, making them great for baby projects. Many whimsical novelty yarns are made of acrylic fibers.

Many of these fibers are blended with each other to incorporate various features. For example, blending a wool with a cashmere fiber will bring the yarn's cost down while still maintaining a delicious softness, or adding a touch of silk to wool will soften it without sacrificing durability.

Eyelash

Ribbon

Chenille

Bouclé

Novelty Yarns

Once you start knitting, it won't be long before you're itching to knit with a sparkly, fluffy, shiny, furry, or otherwise strangely compelling yarn. Novelty yarns can zest up your knitting and offer a wacky diversion from your fisherman woolen sweater project and stockinette stitch hats.

Eyelash: Eyelash yarns have long fibers (like eyelashes, get it?) hanging off a main strand of yarn. As you can imagine, this yarn can knit up into a fun, furry garment.

Ribbon: If you think about it, you can knit with any sort of long strand: string, twine, and yes, even ribbon. Thin ribbon yarns are very popular because they feel great against the skin and can knit up light and spongy or slinky and silky.

Chenille: You've probably had a chenille throw or sweater at some point in your life. Chenille is incredibly comforting and warm and pleasing to the touch. However, it can be a bit tough to knit with, because it has very little "give."

Bouclé: Bouclé yarns are as fun to knit with as the word is to say. This type of yarn features lots of small loops along the yarn. Bouclé knits up very fluffy and is shown off to its best advantage when knit on large needles and with a simple stitch pattern. It can be a little tough to knit with, however, as you can easily knit into a loop of the yarn, rather than a stitch.

Yarn Textures

Marled yarn is made by twisting contrasting colors of yarn together into one yarn, which results in a speckled or obviously multicolored yarn.

Heathered yarns are similar to marled yarns but they are comprised of strands of similarly colored or complementary colored yarns.

Variegated yarns feature a variety of colors within the same ball or skein of yarn. Sometimes they are in the same color family—such as fuchsia, bubble gum, and pale pinks—or could be lots of colors that work together—such as earth tones or cheery primary colors. Some variegated yarns are carefully dyed different colors at different spots in the yarn so that when it's knit up, into a sock, for instance, it creates a pattern, usually of stripes. Cool, huh?

Ply usually indicates the number of strands (singles) spun separately to create yarn; they are then plied together. So 4-ply means that four strands (singles) were used to create one yarn. A single strand of yarn that hasn't been plied with another strand (or more) can render the yarn delicate, unless it's an extremely durable fiber to begin with.

Heathered

Marled

Variegated

KNITTING FOR SOMEONE ELSE

Just because you adore someone and think you know his or her taste doesn't mean that you do.

There's a whole new list of questions to answer before you embark upon a project for a loved one. Just because you adore someone and think you know his or her taste doesn't mean that you do. Unless you shop together on a weekly basis, you might be surprised to find out what he or she actually likes.

Yarn Weights

While each yarn is unique, there are some general guidelines about yarn weights (i.e., how thick or thin the yarn is). Depending on what kind of garment you want to knit, these general terms can steer you in the right direction when choosing your yarn. The Craft Yarn Council of America (CYCA) has developed a numbering system to distinguish basic yarn weights.

Superfine, sock, fingering, or baby weight: (CYCA: 1 Superfine) This very thin fiber is great for knitting lace, socks, and baby garments.

Sportweight: (CYCA: 2 Fine) Slightly thicker than Superfine, sportweight yarns are also suitable for socks and baby projects.

DK: (CYCA: 3 Light) Also called "light worsted," DK yarn is a good lightweight yarn for light garments.

Worsted: (CYCA: 4 Medium) A medium-weight, durable yarn great for a variety of projects.

Bulky, or chunky: (CYCA: 5 Bulky) As the name suggests, bulky yarns are quite thick and are great for heavier sweaters and garments. Paired with a large needle, bulky yarns knit up quickly so you can see results right away.

Super bulky, or super chunky: (CYCA: 6 Super Bulky) This is the big daddy of yarns, and is usually reserved for chunky sweaters and jackets. Large needles are a must when working with this über-thick yarn.

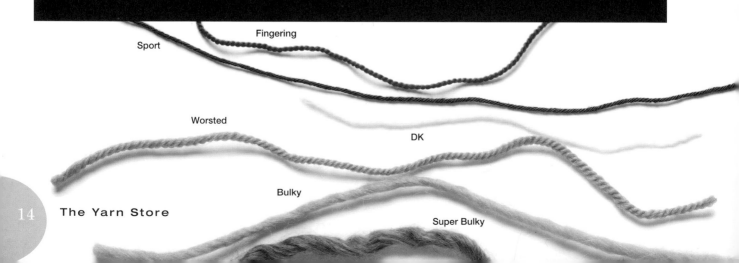

Sport

Fingering

Worsted

DK

Bulky

Super Bulky

Rather than surprise a loved one with your vision, do a bit of sleuthing and ask yourself a few questions:

- ✎ What's the individual's style: conservative, trendy, classic, outrageous?
- ✎ What color does she normally wear?
- ✎ What color flatters him most?
- ✎ Does she wear loose- or snug-fitting clothing?
- ✎ Have you ever seen him take something to the dry cleaner, let alone handwash it?
- ✎ Is she clumsy and prone to spilling?
- ✎ Does he tend to get overheated easily, or is he always chilled?
- ✎ What's her absolute favorite article of clothing?
- ✎ Is he a bit of a dandy or more of a slob?
- ✎ What body part is she most self-conscious about? Proud of?

If you can take her shopping and ask a few subtle questions, all the better. Maybe you assumed that she'd love a tunic sweater because she lives for comfort but after suggesting she try one on, learned that because of her large bust size, she feels like she's wearing a shapeless tent. Hmmm, maybe a fitted cardigan might be a better choice! Don't make assumptions based on your taste and opinions. Even if you think that cobalt-blue scarf makes him look like a movie star, if he hates the color or how it feels against his skin, he'll never show the world how stunning he can look. That scarf will be at the bottom of his underwear drawer, never to see the light of day.

CAN'T FIND A YARN SHOP?

Many craft and variety stores stock basic knitting supplies (check the Yellow Pages or the Internet to find one nearby). While the yarn selection may not be as wide-ranging as a shop specializing in knitting and needlecrafts, you will be able to find the materials you need to get started. Just make sure you are happy with the color and fiber you choose. You'll be spending a lot of time with it!

Reading a Yarn Label

Most yarn labels (which are wrapped around a ball or skein) list a wealth of information and offer guidelines on needle size, gauge, and care instructions.

Weight, usually in grams

Length of yarn in skein, usually in both yards and meters

Fiber content

Recommended **needle size** to achieve a particular **gauge**

Care instructions

Color number and dye lot

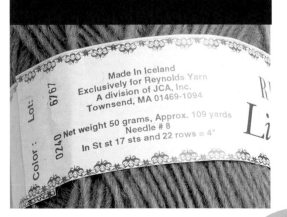

2

The Basics

You navigated the yarn shop and have returned with a bag of supplies. You maybe even have figured out the answers to the questions at right (b, c, d, a, d). Now what?

In knitting, a "stash" is:
a) the secret project you're hiding from a loved one.
b) your surplus yarn collection.
c) a stitch that doesn't look quite right.
d) yarn you purchased on sale.

The two basic knitting stitches are:
a) yarnover and slipstitch.
b) increase and decrease.
c) knit and purl.
d) diamond and pearl.

Yarn should be protected from:
a) moths.
b) moisture.
c) light.
d) all of the above.

Ribbing is achieved by:
a) using an alternating pattern of knits and purls in your rows, such as "knit 2, purl 2."
b) changing yarns every few stitches.
c) twisting the yarn.
d) alternating needle sizes.

When first knitting, you'll feel
a) clumsy.
b) excited.
c) creative.
d) all of the above.

Let's set up a fabulous knitting space that has everything you need within arm's reach, including a space for your new best friend—your "Getting Started" book! You'll then be armed and ready to cast on, knit, and purl—words that still sound like a foreign language—so you can start on your knitting adventure and create a variety of creative but totally "doable" starter projects.

You are understandably eager to get started with your project. Before getting under way, however, carve out a block of time and a quiet spot. Make sure you have good lighting, put on a mellow CD, and place a glass or mug of your favorite beverage within easy reach. Believe me, once you get going, you're not going to want to get up for anything!

And once you get the hang of the basics, you'll be keen to take your knitting on the road. You can use any tote bag to hold your yarn, needles, and pattern, but it's a nice idea to use the bag only for your knitting. Don't be tempted to throw other items in the bag that can snag or stain your project. You put a lot of time and care into your work, so protect it. If the project is small enough, seal your knitting in a Ziploc bag and transfer it to whatever handbag you're using. Take care, however, to keep tabs on it. You can never replace lost or stolen work!

CREATING A KNITTING SPACE AND KNITTING BAG

Don't be tempted to throw items in your yarn bag that can snag or stain your knitting.

Your stash, or collection of yarn, will get bigger and bigger. That's almost a guarantee. Yarn, however, can be damaged by light, moisture, or critters so take preventative measures to protect your stash by placing yarns in sealed plastic bags or containers in a dry, dark place (like the top shelf of a closet). Throw in a sachet to keep the yarn fresh-smelling.

You're armed with the supplies you need for your first project and have prepped the perfect space. So like the name of this handy book says, let's Get Started Knitting!

STORING YOUR STASH

CASTING ON
The first thing you need to do is get the yarn on a needle.

Figure 1. Leave a long tail of yarn.

Figure 2. Place a needle under the bar of yarn in the loop.

Figure 3. Separate the two strands with your thumb and index finger.

The first thing you need to do is get the yarn on a needle. This is called "casting on," and can be done in a couple of ways. My favorite is the **long-tail cast-on.** It gives a very smooth edge and once you get the hang of it, is a speedy way to get your stitches on a needle.

Step 1: Leaving a long tail of yarn (Figure 1)—figure three times the width of what you are knitting; for instance, if you are knitting an 8" (2.5-cm)-wide scarf, start with a 24" (61-cm)-long tail—make a slip-knot, and place it on a needle. To make a slipknot, lay your "tail" of yarn on a flat surface and make a loop near the area where the tail becomes your ball of yarn.

Step 2: Place the tail of yarn under the loop. Still with me?

Step 3: Now place a needle under the bar of yarn within the loop you just made with the tail (Figure 2).

Step 4: Pull both ends of the yarn to complete the slipknot. You now have your first stitch on your needle!

Step 5: From here, it gets a little tricky. Place the needle with the stitch in your right hand. With your left hand, hold the two strands of yarn, with the long tail hanging to your left and the strand attached to the ball to the right. With your right index finger on top of the needle holding the slipknot in place, grab onto the two strands a few inches below the needle with your left hand.

Step 6: Separate the two strands with your thumb and index finger, keeping the yarn taut with your other three fingers (Figure 3). The yarn tail should be around your thumb and the working yarn attached to the ball should be around your index finger.

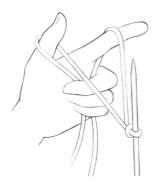

Figure 4. Raise your hand so it's slightly above the needle.

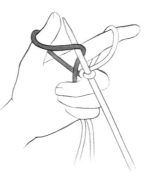

Figure 5. Bring the needle into the loop on your thumb.

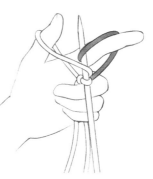

Figure 6. Bring the needle over and back through the loop on your finger.

Step 7: Raise your hand so that it's slightly above the needle (Figure 4). From left to right, bring the needle into the loop created by your thumb (Figure 5).

Step 8: Bring the needle over and back through the loop created by your index finger (Figure 6). Hang in there. You're doing great!

Step 9: Now to finish, with the strand of yarn from your index finger captured, go back through the thumb loop (Figure 7).

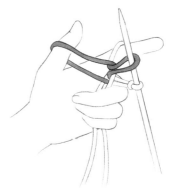

Figure 7. Go back through the thumb loop.

Step 10: Bend your thumb and release the stitch from your thumb. Pull the yarn so you slightly tighten the stitch on the needle. You don't want it to be really tight but it shouldn't be so loose that it slips off the needle or looks uneven.

Congratulations! You have made your first stitch! Repeat the same process until you have the number of stitches on the needle that your pattern specifies. You're now ready to knit!

THE KNIT STITCH

With the knit stitch and the purl stitch in your arsenal, you can pretty much knit anything.

Knitting consists of two basic stitches—the knit and the purl stitch—and with these two in your arsenal, you can pretty much knit anything. So let's start with the mother of them all: **the knit stitch.**

Knit stitches resemble small Vs when knitted across a row.

If you are left-handed like I am, do not make the mistake of trying to learn how to knit left-handed. Learn along with the rest of the righties and you'll make your life a whole lot easier, as patterns are all written in a standard way and assume you are knitting right-handed. You use both hands when knitting so you might was well develop your ambidextrous skills.

Holding the needle with all the stitches in your left hand, you will take your other needle in your right hand. As you knit, you will be transferring stitches from the left needle to the right. When all the stitches are off the left needle, you will switch needles and start the process over again.

How do you hold the needles and the yarn, you ask? There are two methods: **English** and **Continental.** With the English method, the working yarn is loosely wrapped around the little finger of your right hand, passed under the next two fingers, and then held over your index finger. With the Continental method, you hold the yarn taut by wrapping it around your left index finger. Many experienced knitters prefer to use the Continental method, as it's faster once you've gotten the hang of it. For our purposes, we'll focus on the English method.

Step 1: Hold the needle with the cast-on stitches in your left hand, the empty needle in your right hand. Hold the needles a few inches from the tips, between your thumb and first couple of fingers.

Step 2: With the working yarn in back of the needle, insert the right needle into the front of the first stitch (the one closest to the tip) from left to right (Figure 1).

Step 3: Now with your right index finger, bring the yarn between the needles from back to front (Figure 2).

Step 4: With your right hand, pull the right needle—which now has a loop of yarn around it—toward you and through the stitch (Figure 3). Congratulations! You now have a stitch on the right needle! All you need to do to finish the stitch is to slip the old stitch off the left needle. Tug gently on the working yarn to secure the new stitch and voilà! You've just knit your first stitch!

That wasn't so bad, was it?

Repeat this process through the end of the row and you'll have knit your first row! When you have knitted every stitch on the row, you will have an empty needle in your left hand. Swap needles so that the "full" needle is in your left hand and the empty one in your right and do it all over again. Knitting each row back and forth using only the knit stitch is called **garter stitch.** It basically looks like bumpy rows and works great with novelty yarns, since the stitches have a tendency to disappear beneath fluffy or crazy yarn. It doesn't curl at the edges so it's often used for hems and edges of sweaters, cuffs, hats, scarves, and the like.

Knitting each row back and forth using only the knit stitch produces bumpy rows. It is called garter stitch.

Figure 1. Insert the right needle into the front of the first stitch from left to right.

Figure 2. Bring the yarn between the needles from back to front.

Figure 3. Pull the right needle toward you and through the stitch.

THE PURL STITCH

Now that you've mastered the knit stitch, you are most certainly ready to purl. **Purl** stitches look like tiny horizontal chains when knitted across a row.

Step 1: Again, we are going to focus on the English method. Like the knit stitch, start by holding the needle with the stitches in your left hand and the empty needle in your right.

Step 2: Pull the working yarn in front of the needles. Insert the tip of the right needle into the front of the first stitch on the left needle, from right to left (Figure 1).

Step 3: With the yarn in front of the needles, travel around the tip of right needle in a counterclockwise movement, passing between the needles from right to left and back around to the front again (Figure 2).

Figure 1. Insert the right needle into the front of the first stitch from right to left.

Step 4: Pull the right needle, with the loop of working yarn around it, down and back (moving away from you) through the stitch on the left needle (Figure 3). Slip the old stitch off the left needle and tighten the new stitch on the right needle. You have your first purl stitch. Pat yourself on the back but make sure to put down the needles first!

Repeat this process through the end of the row and you'll have purled an entire row! Just like with the knit stitch, when you have purled every stitch on the row, you will have an empty needle in your left hand. Swap needles so that the "full" needle is in your left hand and the empty one in your right and do it all over again.

Note: If you purl every row . . . you also get garter stitch!

Figure 2. Bring the yarn around the tip of the right needle in a counterclockwise movement.

Figure 3. Pull the right needle away from you through the stitch.

The most commonly used stitch pattern is **stockinette stitch.** Stockinette stitch, or St st as it's abbreviated, occurs when you knit one row, purl the next row, and so on. All odd rows might be knitted and all even rows purled. This results in a side of smooth knitting that looks like interlocking vertical Vs when examined up close. This is the side of knit stitches that is usually called the **right side,** or the side that is meant to be seen. The other purled side of your knitting, or the **wrong side,** will look like lots of horizontal bumps and is often hidden from view when the garment is worn.

Stockinette stitch has a tendency to curl at the edges so many patterns include an edge of garter stitch or ribbing to prevent rolling.

STOCKINETTE STITCH

Right Side   Wrong Side

The word "gauge" is enough to scare anyone. It sounds technical and precise, and in some ways it is. But it's also necessary. Checking your gauge, or the size of your stitches, before you start knitting a pattern will make sure you knit a properly sized garment. Everyone knits slightly differently (maybe you knit so tightly that it's hard to slip your needle into a stitch or perhaps you knit really loose stitches) and this affects gauge, as does the yarn and needles you choose to use.

Most patterns tell you the **horizontal gauge** with which the pattern was knit. For instance, on page 36, look at the Ladder Scarf pattern. As easy as it is, it includes gauge. It's listed as 10 stitches = 4" (10 cm). This means that there are 2½ stitches = 1" (2.5 cm). If a gauge doesn't list a stitch pattern, assume that it should be achieved in stockinette stitch. This means that using the yarn and needles recommended in the pattern, you will be knitting 2½ stitches for every inch (2.5 cm) in the width of your knitting. If the project is 6" (15 cm) wide, that means that you'll need to cast on 15 stitches (which, as you'll see, is what the pattern asks you to do). You didn't think you'd need those math skills to knit, did you? Keep a calculator in your knitting bag.

THE GAUGE STAGE

The word "gauge" is enough to scare anyone. It sounds technical and precise, and in some ways it is. But it's also necessary.

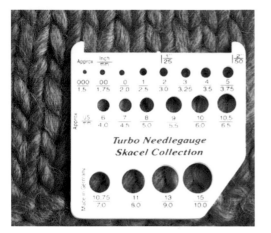

Horizontal Gauge

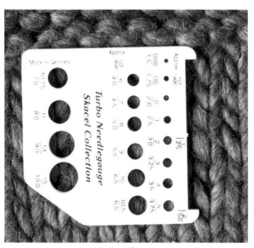

Vertical Gauge

So let's do a trial run. See the photos at left? They are also from the Ladder Scarf.

↪ Do you see the interlocking Vs? That's because it's knit in stockinette stitch. Pick out one complete V. That's one stitch.
↪ We've laid a gauge ruler over the swatch. How many stitches are in 2" (5 cm) of knitting? 5.
↪ Divide that by two and you get 2½ stitches to every 1" (2.5 cm).

The reason that it's wise to measure a bigger area of knitting is that there's less chance for error. If you are knitting on tiny needles with fine yarn, you might have many stitches per inch or centimeters and if you are off by one or two when counting an inch (2.5 cm) of stitches, you could considerably throw off the sizing of your garment. And that would be tragic! But if you check and double check a 4" (10-cm) swatch, even if you are off by one stitch, you will be much closer to an accurate gauge. That's why most patterns will report the gauge over 4" (10 cm) rather than over 1" (2.5 cm).

Sometimes it is necessary to check the **vertical gauge.** For instance, if you are knitting a sweater and the gauge is listed as "20 stitches and 24 rows = 4" (10 cm)" you need to not only to knit 5 stitches to the inch (2.5 cm) across a row, but you need also to try to create a swatch that gives you 6 rows to the inch. If your vertical (row) gauge is too short, you might need to knit more rows than the pattern calls for, or that tunic might start looking a bit cropped. Conversely, if your vertical gauge is too long, a miniskirt might become a maxi when all is said and done. I'm overstating this—usually if you hit your stitch gauge, you'll be in the ballpark on your vertical gauge—but I can't stress enough how important it is to check gauge at the outset and take stock of your knitting throughout the process.

Most sweater patterns include a **schematic** that is a line drawing of the pieces of the garment. Measurements for different sizes point to various parts of the schematic to give you further guidance: body length up to the sleeve, body width, sleeve length and width, neck, etc. Use these handy tools to aid you in your adventures in knitting.

TAKING A RIBBING

Ribbing is used frequently in many garments. A combination of knit and purl stitches (such as "knit 2, purl 2" across each row), ribbing creates vertical rows in your knitting and causes your knitting to expand and contract like an accordion, which allows the garment to fit you snugly but comfortably.

To create a basic rib:

Step 1: Cast on an even number of stitches divisible by 4 and that will allow you to begin the row with knit 2 and end the row with purl 2 (or vice versa). Usually, it's better to end a row with the same stitch type with which it began (which creates symmetry in your project). For example, cast on an even number divisible by 4, *plus 2*, and you can begin and end the row with knit 2 (or purl 2). Casting on 12 stitches for a knit 2, purl 2 rib will have you starting a row with knit stitches and ending the row with purl stitches, or vice versa. Instead, cast on 10 or 14 stitches and you will end a row with 2 stitches of the same stitch type you started the row with.

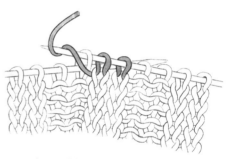

Create ribbing by alternating columns of knit and purl stitches.

Step 2: Knit 2 stitches, purl 2 stitches, then repeat this sequence to the end of the row, ending with knit 2 stitches.

Step 3: Now, on the next row (which will be row 2 and the "wrong side"), purl the purl stitches and knit the knit stitches as they face you. If you can't quite distinguish your purls from your knit stitches yet, don't worry. Just know that the wrong-side stitch pattern will be the opposite of the right-side. For instance, if your pattern tells you to knit 2, purl 2, across row 1 (the right side), ending with knit 2, then for row 2, you will purl 2, knit 2 across the row and end with purl 2. As you continue to do this, you'll start to see the springy vertical rows growing off your needle. Cool, huh?

BINDING OFF

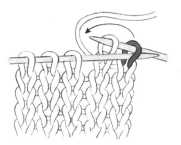

Figure 1. Insert the left needle into the first stitch on the right needle.

Figure 2. Lift the first stitch over the second stitch and off the needle, leaving just one stitch on the right needle.

You made it to the end of your project! Yippee! Well, you can't go around with a needle stuck in the end of your knitting, so you're going to have to **bind off** all the remaining stitches and create an edge to this end of your knitting.

As with most things in knitting, there are several ways to bind off, depending on what kind of edge you want. Some bind-off methods can create delicate, lacy edges; others produce a very even and sturdy edge. For our purposes, we'll cover the most common and easy way to get those stitches off your needles.

Step 1: The first part's easy. If you have reached the last row, just knit two stitches.

Step 2: Insert the left needle into the front of the *first* stitch on the right needle (Figure 1). Pull it over the second stitch and the tip of the needle, so only one stitch is left (Figure 2).

Step 3: It takes 2 stitches on your right needle to bind off 1 stitch. You already have one stitch waiting, so knit another stitch and repeat this process, taking the stitch on the right and pulling it over the second stitch and tip so only one stitch remains on the right needle.

Step 4: Continue this across the row. When you have only one stitch remaining on the right needle, cut the working yarn, leaving a tail of about 6" (15 cm) long. Thread it back through the last stitch, pull to tighten, and weave the remaining yarn (see page 27) into your garment. You've bound off!

Once in a while, you will be called upon to bind off using a different method. If one of the patterns in this book calls for a modified bind-off technique, step-by-step instructions will be included with the pattern.

When you are knitting a garment, even a small one, you will probably need more than one ball or skein of yarn. When you get to the end of one ball, you will need to **join a new ball** to your work. The best way to do this is at the end of a row.

Step 1: Tie the old yarn and new yarn together with a loose knot. Leave a tail of at least 6" (15 cm) that can be woven in later.

Step 2: Start knitting with the new working yarn, making sure to keep the two yarn tails away from your needles.

JOINING A NEW BALL OF YARN

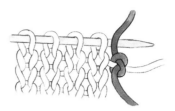

Tie the old yarn and new yarn together with a loose knot.

You've finished your garment, but you've got some nasty strands of yarn hanging here and there. How do you get rid of them? Well, put down the scissors! Clipping excess yarn can lead to unraveling, a sure way to bring a knitter to tears.

Instead, **weave in the yarn ends** into your garment so they are invisible to the naked eye.

To do this, you'll need a **tapestry needle,** which looks like an oversized sewing needle with a blunt tip and a big eye.

Step 1: Thread the yarn tail through the needle's eye. This can be tricky, since yarn can be bulky. **Here's a tip:** Near the end of the tail, fold a couple of inches (5 cm) of yarn over the needle and pull both ends of the yarn taut. Hold the yarn strands tightly between your thumb and index finger just below the needle. Slip the needle from between the yarn strands. Now feed the flattened, bent yarn through the eye. This works like a charm for virtually all yarns. (If your yarn is super bulky and won't fit through a tapestry needle, it may be necessary to weave your yarn ends in with a crochet needle or even by hand.)

WEAVING IN ENDS

Tip: When you are done with your garment and weaving in yarn ends with a tapestry needle, you can actually untie the knot and weave the two ends in separately. Don't worry; nothing will unravel!

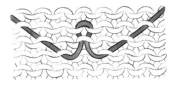

Weave tails into the wrong side of the garment.

Step 2: Weave the tail in and out of a place that's not too visible, such as a seam, the side of the garment, or the wrong side. If you have a tail in the middle of a row, weave the ends diagonally into the "purl bumps" on the wrong side of the knitting. I like to weave up into one stitch and then down into another in the opposite direction, to further ensure that the tail stays put. When you feel the yarn is secure, clip the remaining yarn tail. That's it!

BLOCKING

Always read the yarn label for insight about washing and blocking.

Once you've finished a garment, particularly a sweater, it's often a good idea to block it. **Blocking** is a method of steaming or wetting a garment and reshaping it so the stitches even out throughout the piece. It's the last step to ensuring that you've knit something professional, no matter your level of knitting expertise. Of course, if you are an even knitter and are delighted with your work, there's no need to block it. However, some stitch patterns demand to be blocked, such as lace, so read the following carefully.

It's best to block your pieces before you sew them together. You can smooth out any rough or uneven patches of yarn or knitting before you start assembling your garment.

Many synthetic yarns can be damaged by heat, so avoid steaming them as well as yarns with synthetic fibers blended in. Wool can benefit greatly from blocking. If a woolen garment is a bit too snug, you can reshape it and pin it to your liking when blocking. Cotton, however, doesn't change shape much, so you only need to steam it lightly. Knowing your fiber will allow you to know how much or little to block your finished garments.

Tip: It's best to block your pieces before you sew them together. You can smooth out any rough or uneven patches of yarn or knitting before you start assembling your garment.

To wet-block your work of art

Step 1: Wet the work in a basin of cold water until the entire piece is saturated. Remove it from the basin and gently squeeze out the water. You can also place it flat on a towel and roll up the towel, squeezing the water out of the knitted item in the process. (If your work only needs light blocking, you can spritz it with water to wet it lightly.)

Step 2: Place a towel on a flat surface in which you will be able to stick pins (such as an out-of-the-way carpeted area or a sofa). Lay the wet item flat on the towel and shape it to your liking, smoothing out rough areas or gently pulling on it to enlarge it (some items, like wool shawls, can become significantly larger with blocking). You can leave it this way, checking it occasionally and making adjustments through the drying process, or you can use T-pins or straight pins to affix the knitted item to the towel and area beneath.

Step 3: Allow your item to dry before picking it up and admiring it.

To steam-block your creation

Step 1: Set your iron to the setting appropriate for your type of yarn fiber. Make sure the "steam" setting is on as well.

Step 2: As with wet blocking, pin your garment in the desired shape to a towel on a carpet or sofa. Hold the iron about ½" (1.3 cm) above the knitted area and steam the entire piece (except ribbed areas, which will lose their elasticity if blocked). Slightly reshape the damp knitting as you wish.

Step 3: Allow your item to dry, remove the pins, and enjoy.

Blocking

Yarns that can be steam- or wet-blocked:
- Alpaca
- Linen
- Cashmere
- Wool
- Cotton

Yarns that should be wet-blocked:
- Angora
- Camel hair
- Mohair
- Wool blends
- Acrylic
- Polyester
- Other synthetic yarns

Yarns that don't need blocking:
- Many novelty yarns
- Many fuzzy or textured yarns

Once you've bound off all the stitches and woven in the stray strands, you may be champing at the bit to show off your new creation. Before that happens, however, you may need to "finish" your garment by sewing the individual pieces together.

SEAMING YOUR GARMENT

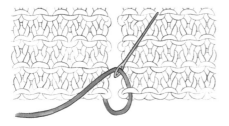

Figure 1. Begin at the bottom edge of the seam.

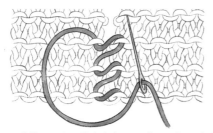

Figure 2. For garter stitch, bring needle up through the purl bump on one side, then the other.

There may come a time, probably sooner than you think, when you will have to sew the pieces of your knitting together to finish a garment (and don't worry—you're sewing the pieces with yarn, not a tiny needle and thread). Maybe it's connecting a sleeve to the body of a sweater, or maybe it's just joining two sides of a leg warmer together. Regardless, **seaming** is really quite painless.

How you sew your pieces together depends on whether you are working a vertical (seaming along the vertical rows in two pieces) or horizontal (seaming along the stitches in the two rows you are joining) seam.

Generally you sew seams with the leftover yarn from your project (or the tail from your cast-on), unless the yarn is highly textured or isn't sturdy. A fine cashmere, for instance, might pull apart when the seam is tightened. Seam, instead, with a sturdy, flat yarn in a color similar to the pieces.

Sewing a vertical seam on garter stitch:
Step 1: Lay the two pieces next to each other, right sides facing up. Thread a tapestry needle with a length of yarn at least three times as long as the area you are sewing.

Step 2: Working from the bottom up, weave the seaming yarn from front to back on the bottom corner of one piece and then, from back to front, bring it through the bottom corner on the other piece (Figure 1). Pull the yarn snugly to join the bottom edges.

Step 3: Insert the needle from bottom to top into the purl bump of a side stitch on one side. Bring the needle up through the bottom edge of the slightly higher stitch on the other piece. Continue sewing on alternate sides in this fashion until you finish the seam (Figure 2). Pull tightly and the two pieces should join seamlessly! Weave the yarn end into the seam for a few inches (or centimeters).

Sewing a vertical seam on stockinette stitch:

Step 1: Lay the two pieces next to each other, right sides (smooth sides) facing up. Thread a tapestry needle with a length of yarn at least three times as long as the area you are sewing.

Step 2: Working from the bottom up, weave the seaming yarn from front to back on the bottom corner of one piece and then, from back to front, bring it through the bottom corner on the other piece as for seaming garter stitch. Pull the yarn snugly to join the bottom edges.

Step 3: Insert the needle under the two horizontal "bars" *between* the first two stitches from the edge on one side of the seam, and then under the two corresponding bars on the other piece. Continue sewing on alternate sides in this fashion (Figure 3), pulling the yarn every so often in the direction of the top of the seam. When finished, pull tightly and the two pieces should join seamlessly! Weave end back into the seam for a few inches.

Sewing a horizontal seam on stockinette stitch:

Step 1: Lay the two pieces next to each other (with one above the other), right sides facing up, bound-off edges side by side and lining up stitch for stitch. Thread a tapestry needle with a length of yarn three times as long as the area you are sewing.

Step 2: To start the seam, *insert the needle from back to front into the center of the V of the stitch just below the bound-off edge of the bottom piece. Insert the needle under the V (the two strands) of the knit stitch on the top piece, then return to the stitch used in the first piece and insert the needle into the center of the same V from front to back. Move to the next V on the bottom piece and repeat from *.

Step 3: Pull the yarn gently as you repeat this process, so that the seam is nearly invisible; it should look like another row of stockinette stitch. Cool, huh? When you reach the end of the bound-off edges, pull gently on your seaming yarn and weave it into the knitted work for a few inches.

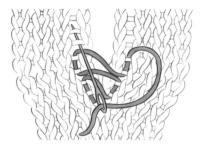

Figure 3. For stockinette stitch, bring needle under two horizontal bars, alternating between the two sides.

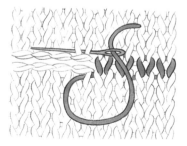

The path of a horizontal seam should mimic a row of knitting.

The Starter Garter Scarf

Design
Lisa R. Myers

Need to know
Cast on (page 18)
Knit stitch (page 20)
Bind off (page 26)
Join a new ball (page 27)
Weave in ends (page 27)

Here's the project that will get your feet wet and whet your appetite for knitting. Knitted in garter stitch, this scarf can be knit at the dimensions listed, or you can choose to make it skinnier by using fewer stitches or longer by knitting more rows. Be as creative and bold as you want to be!

Finished Size
8" (20.5 cm) by 60" (152.5 cm).

Materials

Yarn: CYCA classification: 4 Medium; about 400 yards (360 meters).

Shown here: Plymouth Encore, worsted weight (75% acrylic, 25% wool; 200 yards [180 meters]/100 grams): #9401 light sage, 2 skeins.

Needles: Size 8 (5 mm) straight needles. Adjust needle size if necessary to obtain the correct gauge.

Notions: Measuring tape; tapestry needle.

Gauge
14 stitches = 4" (10 cm) in garter stitch.

Who says your first scarf project has to be a snooze?

In our secret studio, you'll find five fun scarf projects that are just variations on knit and purl stitches. And before you think a project looks too cool to be easy, look through the directions. You might be surprised at how much you already know, and therefore, how many wildly creative projects you can knit up from the get-go.

Scarf

Cast on 28 stitches. Knit each row (i.e., work in garter stitch) until the scarf measures 60" (152.5 cm).

Bind off all stitches loosely.

Finishing

Weave in the loose yarn ends with a tapestry needle.

Check out page 118 for a great way to embellish this scarf.

Muppet Scarf

Design
Lisa R. Myers

Need to know
Cast on (page 18)
Knit stitch (page 20)
Bind off (page 26)
Weave in ends (page 27)

Here's a variation of the Starter Garter Scarf. With this novelty yarn, notice how you can hardly see the actual stitches? Compare it to the Starter Garter Scarf on page 32. Believe it or not, it's the same stitch pattern. We just decreased the number of stitches per row and increased the needle size, since the yarn knits up much bulkier than a plain worsted-weight yarn. When using a particularly fluffy or frou-frou yarn, it doesn't make sense to knit with a complicated or even relatively simple stitch pattern; it gets lost beneath the yarn. Let the stitches take a backseat to the yarn and knit in garter stitch. This uses only one skein of yarn and knits up in a jiffy, so you can spruce up an outfit right away.

Finished Size
4" (10 cm) by 65" (165 cm).
Note: Scarf becomes narrower and longer when worn.

Materials
Yarn: CYCA classification: 6 Super Bulky; about 77 yards (70 meters).
Shown here: Colinettte Firecracker (100% polyamide; 77 yards [70 meters]/100 grams): #21 turquoise, 1 skein.

Needles: Size 15 (10 mm) straight needles. Adjust needle size if necessary to obtain the correct gauge.
Notions: Measuring tape; tapestry needle.

Gauge
8 stitches = 4" (10 cm).

Scarf

Cast on 8 stitches. Knit each row (i.e., work garter stitch) until the scarf measures about 65" (165 cm) or until yarn is almost finished, leaving just enough to bind off. *Note:* As the knitting progresses the scarf becomes longer, and you'll notice that the width begins to narrow as the weight of the yarn lengthens the work. To determine the actual knitted length during the making, gently stretch the width back to 4" (10 cm) before measuring for length.

Bind off all stitches loosely.

Finishing

Weave in the yarn loose ends with a tapestry needle.

Ladder Scarf

Design

Lisa R. Myers

Need to know

Cast on (page 18)
Knit stitch (page 20)
Purl stitch (page 22)
Bind off (page 26)
Join a new ball (page 27)
Weave in ends (page 27)

This scarf shows how creative you can be using basic stockinette stitch, which is just knitting one row and purling the next. In our Ladder Scarf, we've mixed things up a bit to create a reversible scarf that has no right or wrong side because you are knitting a block in stockinette stitch and then knitting a block of reverse stockinette stitch. Sound tricky? Don't worry; we'll walk you through it step by step.

Finished Size

6" (15 cm) by 66" (167.5 cm).

Materials

Yarn: CYCA classification: 6 Super Bulky; about 198 yards (181 meters).

Shown here: JCA/Reynolds Blizzard (65% alpaca, 35% acrylic; 66 yards [59 meters]/ 100 grams): #43 magenta, 3 skeins.

Needles: Size 15 (10 mm) straight needles. Adjust needle size if necessary to obtain the correct gauge.

Notions: Measuring tape; tapestry needle.

Gauge

10 stitches = 4" (10 cm) in stockinette stitch.

Scarf

Cast on 15 stitches. Knit in stockinette stitch (knit right-side rows; purl wrong-side rows) for 10 rows.

On the next row (11th row), purl. You will have just purled two rows consecutively. See what this does? It switches the pattern so that you are now knitting in reverse stockinette stitch. The purl bumps are now on the smooth side of the work, and the smooth knit stitches are on the former bumpy side. Continue in this pattern for the next 9 rows. After purling row 11, knit row 12, purl row 13, and so on until you knit row 20. You have now knit a reverse version of the first block.

Knit row 21 and continue in stockinette stitch until row 30, then work in reverse stockinette stitch until row 40, and so on until your scarf measures 66" (167.5 cm).

Bind off all stitches loosely.

Finishing

Weave in the loose yarn ends with a tapestry needle.

Check out page 111 if you'd like to add a colorful fringe.

Sunset Strips Scarf

Design
Courtney Kelley

Need to know
Cast on (page 18)
Knit stitch (page 20)
Bind off (page 26)
Join a new ball (page 27)
Weave in ends (page 27)

Here's another creative use of garter stitch! This time you are knitting the scarf lengthwise, casting on a boatload of stitches. Each row will take awhile but you don't have nearly as many rows to knit up!

Finished Size
About 62½" (159 cm) by 7" (18 cm)

Materials
Yarn: CYCA classification: 4 Medium; about 109 yards (105 meters) each in 4 colors.
Shown here: Classic Elite Inca Alpaca (100% alpaca; 109 yards [105 meters]/50 grams): #1109 Peruvian earth, #1135 CalaCala moss, #1146 island of the sun, and #1155 harvest bounty, 1 skein each.

Needles: Size 8 (5 mm) 24" (60 cm) circular needle. Adjust needle size if necessary to obtain the correct gauge.
Notions: Measuring tape; tapestry needle.

Gauge
16 stitches = 4" (10 cm) in garter stitch.

Note

If you want to make fringe (see page 111), cut the fringe strands first to make sure you have enough yarn for the fringe. Then just knit each color until you run out of it, changing colors with each ball.

Color Sequence

- island of the sun (color A)
- Peruvian earth (color B)
- harvest bounty (color C)
- CalaCala moss (color D)

Scarf

Cast on 250 stitches with color A (blue). Knit every row for 18 rows or until you run out of yarn. It takes a good length of yarn to complete one row so as you near the end of a skein, make sure you have a few yards left for the last row. If not, join a new yarn at the beginning of a row and just leave a long tail from the first yarn to weave in later.

Join color B and work as above for the same number of rows, then repeat for each additional color (color C, then color D). Remember to always join a new ball at the beginning of a row, never mid-row.

Bind off when all four colors have been worked, keeping in mind that you will need LOTS of yarn to bind off. Leave roughly 3 times the width to bind off with, which in this case is about 5 to 6 yards.

Finishing

Weave in the loose yarn ends with a tapestry needle.

Taking a Ribbing Scarf

This handsome scarf is a perfect basic for both men and women. It's also a great introduction to ribbing: in no time, you'll be counting stitches and moving your yarn from the back (for knit stitches) to the front (for purl stitches) with ease and confidence.

Finished Size

5" (12.5 cm) by 71" (180 cm), with ribbing relaxed, not stretched.

Materials

Yarn: CYCA classification: 5 Bulky; about 375 yards (343 meters).

Shown here: Brown Sheep Lamb's Pride Bulky (85% wool, 15% mohair; 125 yards [114 meters]/100 grams): #M14 sunburst gold, 3 skeins.

Needles: Size 10½ (6.5 mm) straight needles. Adjust needle size if necessary to obtain the correct gauge.

Notions: Measuring tape; tapestry needle.

Gauge

12 stitches = 4" (10 cm) in stockinette stitch.

Design
Lisa R. Myers

Need to know
Cast on (page 18)
Knit stitch (page 20)
Purl stitch (page 22)
Ribbing (page 25)
Bind off (page 26)
Join a new ball (page 27)
Weave in ends (page 27)

Scarf

Cast on 26 stitches.

Row 1: *Knit 2, purl 2; repeat from * to the last 2 stitches, knit 2.

Row 2: Purl 2, *knit 2, purl 2; repeat from * to the end of row. Repeat Rows 1 and 2 until work measures 71" (180 cm) from cast-on.

Bind off all stitches.

Finishing

Weave in the loose yarn ends with a tapestry needle.

Fast Favorite Wrap or Poncho

Versatility is the key to this project. Seam it up and you have a hip poncho. Leave it be and you have a funky, warm wrap. You might decide you want both, so knit up a couple in this warm bouclé yarn. Whatever the case, you'll be reaching for this again and again and wondering how you ever lived without it.

Design
Grace Anna Robbins

Need to know
Cast on (page 18)
Knit stitch (page 20)
Bind off (page 26)
Join a new ball (page 27)
Weave in ends (page 27)

Finished Size
Wrap: 17½" (44.5 cm) by 52" (132 cm).
Poncho: About 27" (68.5 cm) at point.

Materials
Yarn: CYCA classification: 5 Bulky and 6 Super Bulky; about 420 yards (384 meters).
Shown here: Plymouth Yarns Alpaca Bouclé (90% alpaca, 10% nylon; 70 yards [64 meters]/50 grams): #20, 6 skeins.

Needles: Size 10½ (6.5 mm) straight needles. Adjust needle size if necessary to obtain the correct gauge.
Notions: Measuring tape; tapestry needle.

Gauge
10 stitches = 4" (10 cm) in garter stitch.

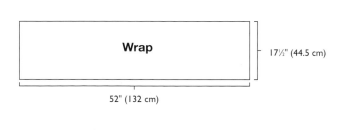

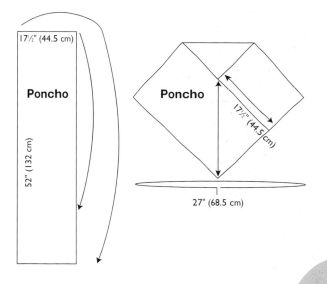

Binding Off Mid-Row

When you bind off stitches mid-row between groups of live stitches, there will always be 1 stitch remaining on the right needle after the bind off; this stitch counts as the first stitch in the next set of instructions. Example: If the next same-row instructions specify "knit 5 after the bind-off," you'll already have 1 live stitch on the right needle; to complete the knit 5, you only need to knit 4 more stitches. When you're instructed to bind off again in the same row, re-member to knit 2 more stitches before beginning the bind-off (it takes 2 stitches on the right needle to bind off 1 stitch).

Note

The work will be narrower than indicated in finished measurements until the stitches are dropped to form the open ladder work.

Wrap or Poncho

Cast on 39 stitches.

Knit every row (i.e., work garter stitch) until piece measures 52" (132 cm) from cast-on.

Bind off row: Bind off 3 stitches, knit 3, bind off 6 stitches, knit 3, bind off 9 stitches, knit 3, bind off 11 stitches (1 stitch remains on the right needle, this is the 12th stitch), cut yarn leaving 6" (15-cm) tail and thread through the remaining 12th stitch, pull tail to tighten and secure the bind-off.

*Slip 1 stitch off needle, cut the 2nd stitch, taking care not to cut the work below the stitch, insert the needle into the 3rd stitch, pulling upward so the stitch becomes a larger and larger loop (making the previous stitches drop) and eventually pulls out. You'll have a short yarn tail at each edge of the dropped stitches. Working one yarn tail at a time, thread the tails on the tapestry needle and weave in along several bound-off stitches to secure. Repeat from * across each group of 3 knit stitches. The dropped stitches will form the open ladder-work pattern.

Yes, you intentionally drop the stitches—the stitch will come off the needle and start to unravel. In this case, it's a good thing. Because the stitches generally want to stay put, after a row or two, you may need to coax them a bit. Pull on them and stretch the garment so the stitches vertically unravel, leaving a cool stripe-y pattern in the garment.

Finishing

To make a wrap
 Weave in the yarn ends with a tapestry needle.

To make a poncho
Position the rectangle so the 12-stitch bound-off section will be the lower edge of the poncho. Working on the wrong side, and with yarn threaded on tapestry needle, take the cast-on edge and place it next to the long side (see schematic, page 41), then whipstitch (see box below) them together (you will be sewing the yarn strands from the dropped stitches to edge stitches in some areas). The seam is complete when you've reached the end of the cast-on edge. Weave in all yarn ends to wrong side of work. Turn work to right side.

Whipstitch

Use a whipstitch to sew the cast-on edge to the long end of the knitted piece. To work a whipstitch, insert threaded tapestry needle at right angle through a stitch on one piece, then through a corresponding  stitch on the other piece. Pull stitches together to join the two pieces firmly but not so tight that the pieces pucker.

Super Hero Hand Huggers

Design

Courtney Kelley

Need to know

Cast on (page 18)

Knit stitch (page 20)

Purl stitch (page 22)

Ribbing (page 25)

Bind off (page 26)

Weave in ends (page 27)

Seaming (page 29)

Hand huggers, or wrist warmers, are a fun and cozy way to perk up your outfit. The yummy Lush yarn we used is perfect for a "knit 1, purl 1" rib and perfect for creating wrist warmers fit for any super heroine.

Finished Size

6" (15 cm) in circumference and 6½" (16.5 cm) long.

Note: Ribbing is very elastic, and will stretch another 1–2" (2.5–5 cm).

Materials

Yarn: CYCA classification: 4 Medium; 123 yards (112 meters).

Shown here: Classic Elite Lush (50% angora, 50% wool; 123 yards [112 meters]/ 50 grams): #4468 madder, 1 skein.

Optional: About 4 yards (3.5 meters) of contrast color yarn for blanket stitch edging.

Needles: Size 7 (4.5 mm) straight needles. Adjust needle size if necessary to obtain the correct gauge.

Notions: Measuring tape; tapestry needle.

Gauge

18 stitches = 4" (10 cm) in stockinette stitch.

Hand Hugger (make 2)

Cast on 40 stitches on a size 8 (5 mm) straight needle. Work back and forth in rows in knit 1, purl 1 rib until piece measures 6½" (16.5 cm) from cast-on.

Bind off all stitches.

With yarn threaded on a tapestry needle, sew a seam from the cast-on edge to about 3" (7.5 cm) from the top edge. Cut yarn. Leave a 1" (2.5-cm) space for thumb, and seam the rest of the way to the top.

Finishing

Weave in the loose yarn ends with a tapestry needle.

If you like, embellish the edges with blanket stitch (see box below) in a contrasting color.

Blanket Stitch

Cut a length of yarn five times longer than the area you are edging. Working along the edge closest to you (either cast-on or bind-off) insert the needle from back to front about 2 rows up from the edge, leaving a 4" (10-cm) tail on the wrong side to weave in later. *Holding the working yarn along the lower edge, move to the right and the next knit stitch (skipping the purl stitch), and 2 rows up from the edge, insert the needle into the stitch from front to back, bring the needle down toward the lower edge, passing over the yarn at the lower edge and pull gently to close. Repeat from * until you reach the beginning. On the last stitch, pull the yarn through the lower edge of the first stitch and connect the first and last stitches together. Turn work to wrong side and weave in the loose yarn ends through several stitches.

Scrappy Leg Warmers

Design

Courtney Kelley

Need to know

Cast on (page 18)

Knit stitch (page 20)

Purl stitch (page 22)

Ribbing (page 25)

Bind off (page 26)

Join a new ball (page 27)

Weave in ends (page 27)

Seaming (page 29)

Stop wondering what to do with all the leftover scraps of yarn in your stash. Put them to good (and creative) use in these kicky leg warmers. We used the remaining yarn from the other projects in this book but feel free to knit in your own unique collection.

Finished Size

12½" (31.5 cm) wide in non-ribbed area and about 16" (40.5 cm) long.

Materials

Yarn: CYCA classification: 4 Medium. Scraps of leftover worsted-, afghan-, or Aran-weight yarn in your stash. If you mix in finer yarns, keep the stripes no wider than 2 rows each, and intersperse between the thicker yarns; or hold 2 finer yarns together and work as one.

Needles: Size 7 (4.5 mm) or 8 (5 mm) straight needles.

Notions: Measuring tape; tapestry needle.

Gauge

The gauge will vary, depending on the yarn you use. You are not changing needle size, but you are changing yarns, and different yarn weights will produce a different gauge, but that's part of the fun!

Leg warmer (make 2)

Cast on 58 stitches. Work in knit 1, purl 1 rib until piece measures 2" (5 cm) from cast-on.

Change to stockinette stitch (knit right-side rows; purl wrong-side rows) and work in stripes, changing yarns and colors whenever you feel like it. Make each leg warmer different or the same, depending on your mood. If you want to match the leg warmers, take notes of how many rows you knitted with each yarn.

When your work reaches desired length from the knee to the foot, either work 2" (5 cm) more of knit 1, purl 1 rib, or make hem as follows:

Pick a worsted-weight yarn from your scraps that is nice and smooth (such as Plymouth Encore). Having just finished a wrong-side (i.e., the purl side) row, attach the yarn you picked and purl 1 more row on the right side (the knit side). This creates a purl ridge on the knit side of the work, making it easier and more attractive to fold the work to the wrong side later, for a hem. Continuing in this yarn, purl 1 row again (on the wrong side)! Work stockinette stitch (knit right-side rows; purl wrong-side rows) for 2" (5 cm) more. Bind off all stitches. With yarn (any color) threaded on a tapestry needle, and right sides facing you, sew back seam together using the vertical invisible seam, carefully matching stripes. Weave in yarn ends along wrong side of seam.

Top Hem

Fold the top edge to the wrong side of work along the purl ridge. With yarn threaded on a tapestry needle, sew the bind-off edge to the inside of the legwarmer, 2" (5 cm) from the purl ridge for the hem.

Finishing

Weave in the loose yarn ends with a tapestry needle.

Handwash your Scrappy Leg Warmers like you would any woolen handknits: in cool water with no wringing or agitation. Lay flat to dry.

3

The Next Level

Knitting in the round is:

a) a knitting circle that meets in an Elizabethan theater.

b) the most common way to knit hats.

c) a communal project that gets passed from one knitter to another.

d) knitting from a ball of yarn.

The term "Fair Isle" comes from:

a) a multicolored design created by knitters in the Shetland Islands.

b) an innovative fair-trade agreement, negotiated by members of a fiber co-operative on the island of Mauritius.

c) a dance that originated in Ireland in the late 1950s.

d) a Norse legend involving two lovers lost at sea.

"St st" in a pattern stands for:

a) start stitch.

b) still standing.

c) stockinette stitch.

d) state store.

Increasing the number of stitches in a row is necessary when knitting:

a) sleeves.

b) shaped sweaters.

c) a triangular shawl.

d) all of the above.

Decreasing the number of stitches in a row is necessary when knitting:

a) a rectangular scarf.

b) a square pillow.

c) wrist warmers.

d) none of the above.

Answers: b, a, c, d, d.

By now, you have probably knit a scarf or two (good job!) and are itching to learn a few new techniques to add to your growing knitting skill set, not to mention move on to more varied projects. After all, how many scarves do you, your family, and friends *really* need? Okay, don't answer that. The next step is to learn how to increase and decrease, which will help you create all sorts of shaped garments—hats, shawls, capes, skirts, and, yes, sweaters—and to knit in the round, which will allow you to knit tubular pieces for hats, sweaters, mittens, and the like.

When working with a stitch pattern or different yarns, a pattern might call for you to **place marker** (or "pm," if it's abbreviated). This means that you should place a ring marker between particular stitches on a needle. **Ring markers** help separate different stitch patterns or areas of color. Some patterns will tell you to mark a particular stitch. In this case, you want to attach a **safety pin** or **split-ring marker** into the actual stitch (do not put it on the needle).

When using a marker *between* stitches, it is important to slide it from one needle to the other, much like a slip stitch (see page 50). Do not work into the marker with yarn, or it may wind up knitted into your fabric and not keeping track of your stitch pattern any longer. However, if you are using the ring marker to indicate a particular stitch, such as the center stitch in an expanding shawl, you attach the marker into the actual stitch. To ensure that it doesn't get knit into the garment, use split-ring or safety-pin markers that can be easily removed.

PLACING MARKERS

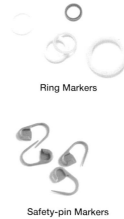

Ring Markers

Safety-pin Markers

SLIP STITCH

The slip stitch sounds like what it is: a stitch that is slipped or moved from the left needle to the right needle without working into the stitch.

Slip a stitch purlwise.

Slip a stitch knitwise.

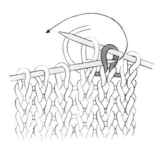

Pass a slipped stitch over (a knitted stitch).

The **slip stitch,** like many other techniques in knitting, sounds like what it is. Basically, you are just slipping or moving a stitch from the left needle to the right needle without working into the stitch. (This creates a denser fabric, which is great for projects like socks.) Sometimes the instructions will say to slip some stitches onto a holder to be worked later. If it doesn't say otherwise, slip the stitch purlwise, unless the slipped stitch is part of a decrease, or the instructions specify otherwise. Here's how:

To slip a stitch purlwise

Step 1: Insert your right needle purlwise (from right to left) into the next stitch on the left needle.

Step 2: Remove the left needle from the stitch. Leave the stitch on the right needle and continue to knit in pattern. Voilà!

To slip a stitch knitwise

Step 1: Insert your right needle knitwise into the next stitch on the left needle. Then work as step 2 above.

Pass slipped stitch over

Also known as "psso," this technique is often used as a decrease method in some openwork patterns, as well as other patterns. To do it, you will probably be asked to slip a stitch, knit or purl one stitch, and then pass the slipped stitch over (abbreviated as "sl 1, k1, psso"). You now know how to slip a stitch, you have knitting and purling down cold, so what do you do about the "psso" notation? Well, it's a bit like a bind-off stitch: with your left needle, lift the slipped stitch (the second from the tip), pull it up and over the stitch you just knitted or purled, and drop it off the needle. You have, in essence, decreased a stitch. Cool, eh?

In your knitting, you will sometimes be asked to knit into the back of a stitch. Huh, you ask? Well, let's break it down.

You already know how to work the standard knit and purl stitches by inserting the right needle into the *front* loop of stitches held on the left needle. But sometimes the pattern designer wants a different stitch effect, and you will be asked to **knit into the back loop.** To do this, insert your right-hand needle into the back loop (the one behind the needle) of the stitch from right to left, and knit as usual. Make sense?

This works the same way for the purl stitch. However, it's a little trickier to purl into the back loop, and takes practice.

To **purl into the back loop,** with yarn in front, insert the tip of your right-hand needle into the back loop of the stitch from the far back to the front (think of coming through the back door of the back loop), then purl the stitch as usual. Check out the illustrations to see the differences.

KNITTING INTO THE FRONT OR BACK OF A STITCH

Front loop

Knit into the front loop

Purl into the front loop

Back loop

Knit into the back loop

Purl into the back loop

INCREASES

Berets, sleeves, shawls, and many other garments require increases to get the proper shaping.

As you progress in your knitting, there will come a time when it's necessary to add stitches at the beginning, end, or somewhere in the middle of a row in order to widen your knitting. Berets, sleeves, shawls, skirts, and many other garments require **increases** to get the proper shaping. There are several ways to increase, depending on the effect you want.

Increase in an existing stitch

One method of adding stitches is to simply knit or purl into a stitch twice. This is an easy way to add stitches, but not the most invisible method; in stockinette stitch one stitch looks the same as the other knit (or purl) stitches, and the increase (made by working into the back loop) forms a small bump that looks a little like a purl stitch with a tiny gap below it. When directions call for you to increase this way, it will say knit into the front and back of the next stitch (k1f&b, k1fb, or kfb). You can also do this purlwise (p1f&b, p1fb, or pfb).

Knit into the front loop of a stitch, then knit into the back loop of the same stitch.

Step 1: Knit into the front of a stitch like you normally would: wrap the yarn around the right needle and bring your right needle (the one carrying the wrapped yarn) through the loop of the old stitch.

Step 2: Before you slip the old stitch off the left needle, bring your right needle to the back and knit into the back loop of the same old stitch on the left needle. Slip the old stitch off the left needle. Voilà! You have two stitches where there had been only one.

Backward loop

Loop the yarn and place it on the needle backward so it doesn't unwind.

Loop the yarn around your thumb and place the twisted loop on the needle.

Make 1

Another great way to add stitches is to create a stitch between two existing stitches, by lifting the bar of yarn between them and basically creating a new stitch. Make 1 increases are the most invisible of the increase techniques and are referred to as "m1" or "M1" when abbreviated in patterns.

Figure 1. Lift the horizontal strand between the stitches on the needles.

Step 1: Insert the left needle from front to back underneath the running strand of yarn between the stitch on your right needle and the first stitch on the left needle (Figure 1).

Step 2: Now place the tip of the right needle through the back loop of this new "stitch" and knit it as you would any other stitch. Wrap yarn around the right needle and pull it through the loop you just created (Figure 2).

Figure 2. Knit the lifted strand through the back loop.

You can also work the make 1 purlwise.

Yarnover

Yarnovers are a great way to increase the number of stitches in a row or round and create an open, lacy look to your knitting. Basically, a yarnover—or "yo" as it's abbreviated in patterns—is just what it says.

To make a yarnover between two knit stitches, bring the working yarn to the front between the needle tips so that it is between two knit stitches, one on each needle. Lay the working yarn over the right needle so that it's now in back. Insert the right needle into the next stitch on the left needle, wrap the yarn around the tip of the right needle (shown at right), then bring it through the loop of the left stitch and slip the old stitch off the left needle. You now have created an additional stitch.

Yarnover between two knit stitches.

Yarnover between two purl stitches.

When making a yarnover between two purl stitches (sometimes referred to as "yarn around needle"), begin with the yarn in front, then take it over the right needle to the back and return to the front again, bringing the yarn between the needle tips. Insert the right needle into the next purl stitch on the left needle purlwise, wrap the yarn over the right needle and finish the stitch the same as making a purl stitch.

DECREASES
Like increases, there are a number of ways to decrease.

Just as you need to increase in many patterns, you will also need to **decrease** the number of stitches in rows or rounds when shaping hats, sweaters, mittens, socks, and the like. Like increases, there is more than one way to decrease. Some methods cause the stitches to lean to the right; others cause them to lean to the left. Many stitch patterns will specify a particular type of decrease, so it's handy to know them all. For instance, many patterns will specify a particular type of decrease to shape the right armhole and another type to shape the left armhole.

Knit two together
Abbreviated "k2tog" in patterns, knitting two stitches together is a speedy way to decrease the number of stitches in your knitting. This type of decrease slants to the right.

Knit two stitches together (k2tog).

Step 1: With the working yarn in back, insert the tip of the right needle first into the second stitch on the left needle, then into the first stitch on the left needle in one smooth movement.

Step 2: Wrap the working yarn around the right needle and pull the strand through the center of both stitches. Slip the two stitches off the left needle. You now have one stitch left where there were two.

Purl two together

When a pattern says "p2tog," you simply purl two stitches together as if they were one.

Slip, slip, knit

This decrease leans—you guessed it!—to the left. Abbreviated as "ssk" (or ssp, if you are purling), a slip, slip, knit decrease involves passing two stitches to the right needle and then knitting them together from the right needle. Here's how:

Step 1: Make sure the working yarn is in the back. Using the tip of the right needle, transfer the first stitch on the left needle to the right needle knitwise. Do not knit or purl or do anything to it, other than pass it from one needle to the other. Do the same with the next stitch on the left needle. You now have two slipped stitches on your right needle.

Step 2: Insert the tip of the left needle into the front loops of the two slipped stitches, wrap the yarn around the right needle and pull the strand through both slipped stitches. Now slip the two old slipped stitches off the left needle. Again, you have one stitch remaining on the right needle.

Knit the slipped stitches together through their back loops.

Things are really starting to get interesting. Your knitting vocabulary and skill level are growing by leaps and bounds. You should now have the confidence to knit a project with **cables.** Nearly everything in knitting is a variation on the knit stitch and the purl stitch, and cables are no exception.

While there are some variations in cables depending on the stitch pattern and garment you are knitting, there are commonalities. Cables are frequently knit on the stockinette (or right) side but, to call attention to and set off the cable pattern, you usually purl a few stitches on either side of the cabled section.

INCREASING YOUR "CABLE"-BILITIES

To make a cable, you knit the stitches in a row out of order.

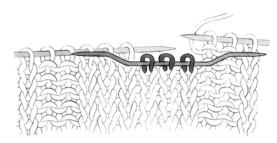

Figure 1. Slip three stitches onto a cable needle.

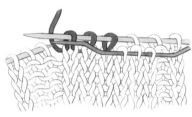

Figure 2. Knit the next three stitches.

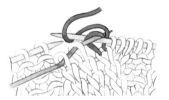

Figure 3. Knit the three stitches on the cable needle.

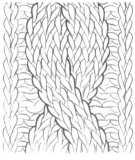

Figure 4. Finished cable.

To make a cable you knit the stitches in a row out of order. In other words, you might knit stitches 13, 14, and 15 before knitting stitches 10, 11, and 12. How do you do this, you ask?

Excellent question! Well, when you get to stitches 10, 11, and 12, you place them on another needle (called a **cable needle,** abbreviated "cn") while you knit the next three stitches on the left needle. Then you pick up the cable needle in your left hand and knit them onto the right needle. Make sense? Let's try it, step by step, assuming that you're working a six-stitch cable every sixth row of knitting.

Step 1: When you get to a cable row in your pattern (the sixth row in this example), work in the stitch pattern listed until you get to the group of six cable stitches.

Step 2: Slip three stitches from the left needle onto a cable needle and, depending on what the pattern calls for, push them to the back of the knitting or pull them to the front (Figure 1).

Step 3: Knit the next three stitches from the left needle to the right (Figure 2).

Step 4: Now for the fun part. Put down the left needle and take hold of your cable needle. Knit the right, middle, and left stitch from your cable needle onto the right needle (Figure 3). Knit the rest of the row according to the pattern. Can you see the twist? Cool, huh?

Step 5: Continue knitting in the cable pattern. After completing a few cable rows (the 6th, 12th, 18th row, etc.), you'll really see the pattern take shape and feel your confidence soaring (Figure 4).

As you might have guessed, cables can be worked purlwise as well.

Many knitters are hesitant about **knitting in the round,** that is, using circular needles to produce seamless tubular knitting. But in fact, it's a snap and has advantages over knitting flat with straight needles. For one thing, you never mix up the right side and the wrong side. If you want to knit a hat with stockinette stitch, for instance, you never have to purl since the right side is always what's showing and being worked. You just keep knitting with knit stitches round and round. Needless to say, that hat will be done in a jiffy!

To knit in the round, you need circular needles that will provide the circumference for the garment you're knitting—a 24" (60-cm) circular needle will be fine for the body of a sweater but way too long for a hat. Conversely, it will be hard to fit all the stitches you'll need for a poncho on a 16" (40-cm) circular needle. The pattern will always spell out what size and length circular needle is recommended to achieve the proper gauge and circumference.

Step 1: To knit in the round, cast on the recommended number of stitches, just like you would on a straight needle.

Step 2: Make sure all of the cast-on stitches are hanging below the needle and are not twisted around the needle.

Step 3: Now hold one needle tip in each hand, this time with the end of the needle connected to the working yarn (i.e., the end of the cast-on row) in your right hand.

Step 4: Depending on what stitch the pattern calls for, knit or purl into the first stitch on the left-hand needle (i.e., the first stitch that was cast on). Again, be careful not to twist the stitches in the cast-on row. All stitches should be hanging below the needle. After this first connecting stitch is made, knitting the rest of the row (or round, as they are called when knitting in the round) should be business as usual. Knit

KNITTING IN THE ROUND
When joining your stitches to knit in the round, make sure all stitches are hanging below the needle.

Join stitches for circular knitting by working the first stitch casted on.

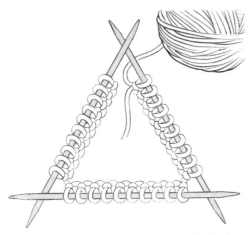

Figure 1. Divide the stitches among three (or four) double-pointed needles.

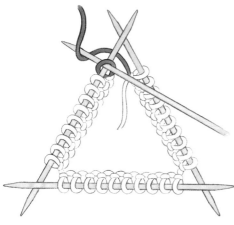

Figure 2. Join for circular knitting by working the first cast-on stitch.

and/or purl in the required stitch pattern to finish the round. Many patterns ask that you place a **stitch marker** (a small ring) on the needle to help you keep track of the first stitch of the round.

Double-pointed needles

We've talked a bit about double-pointed needles but haven't really mentioned how to use them.

Double-pointed needles come in sets of four or five and allow you to knit smaller pieces, such as socks, wrist warmers, and the crowns of hats, in the round. When working in the round, here's how to maneuver "dpn's."

Step 1: Cast on the number of stitches detailed in the pattern onto one double-pointed needle or a straight needle of the same diameter. Divide the stitches as evenly as possible among three or four double-pointed needles (Figure 1).

Step 2: Being careful not to twist the cast-on edge, lay the three needles in a triangle (or four needles in a square), so that the cast-on edge faces the inside. Using the fourth (or fifth) double-pointed needle, knit into the first cast-on stitch, thereby joining the work (Figure 2). Knit or purl as usual to the end of the needle. When that needle becomes empty, switch it to your right hand and use it to knit the stitches on the next needle. Continue in this fashion. While it might seem you are knitting in the triangle or square, when your work comes off the needle, it will be tubular. I swear.

While we won't be doing much color work (that is, knitting with different-colored yarns) in this book, it's helpful to know the two chief types of knitting with multiple yarn colors.

Fair Isle, a knitting method that originated in the Shetland Islands, incorporates bands of repeated multicolored geometric motifs. Sweaters often use this technique around the shoulders and neckline, but Fair Isle patterns can also be used in hats, mittens, gloves, socks, leg warmers, and anything that only shows the right side of the knitting. Strands of yarn are carried loosely on the wrong side of the knitting until the pattern calls for it, so the wrong side of the knitting can often look messy. The result on the right side, however, can be both traditional and stunning.

Intarsia is another fun way to incorporate color into your knitting. With this method, you knit isolated blocks of color (as in the Intarsia Pocket on page 116). You might use intarsia to make a sweater that has a star on the front of it. It could also be used to knit a sweater or blanket with a design of interlocking squares or triangles or even circles. Unlike Fair Isle knitting, you do not carry the yarn along the back of your work. You just drop the color you are knitting with and start with a new color. For a seamless transition, you should twist the old and new yarns. Drop the old yarn, then pick up the new yarn from *under* the old, and begin working the next stitches according to the instructions.

If you'd like to add in some color with minimal effort, you can easily do a scarf with stripes (like the Sunset Strips Scarf, on page 38) of color or edge a hat or sweater with a different colored yarn to zest up your creations. Easier yet, choose a variegated yarn for your project and infuse your work with multiple colors without breaking a sweat.

COLOR YOUR WORLD

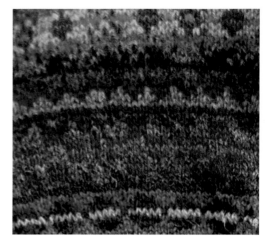

Fair Isle incorporates bands of repeated
multicolored geometric motifs.

Intarsia involves isolated blocks of color.

The Pillow Case

Design

Lisa R. Myers

Need to know

Cast on (page 18)

Knit stitch (page 20)

Purl stitch (page 22)

Bind off (page 26)

Join a new ball (page 27)

Weave in ends (page 27)

Whipstitch (page 43)

Place markers (page 49)

While making garments is a blast, you can also make all sorts of knitted items for your home as well. This checkered throw pillow is knit with a suede-like yarn that feels fabulous to the touch. If you prefer, knit one panel and use it flat as a placemat. Remember, the possibilities are endless when it comes to the wide world of knitting!

Finished Size

12" (30.5 cm) by 12" (30.5 cm).

Materials

Yarn: CYCA classification: 4 Medium; about 360 yards (329 meters).

Shown here: Berroco Suede (100% nylon; 120 yards [111 meters]/50 grams): #3704 wrangler, 3 skeins.

Needles: Size 7 (4.5 mm) straight needles. Adjust needle size if necessary to obtain the correct gauge.

Notions: Stitch markers; measuring tape; tapestry needle; 12" (30.5-cm) pillow form.

Gauge

20 stitches = 4" (10 cm) in stockinette stitch.

Note

For this pattern, we are going to introduce some abbreviations you'll find common in knitting patterns. When you see "k," it means to knit, "p" means to purl. Easy, right? When it says "k17," it means to knit 17 stitches. When we say "p1," it means to purl 1 stitch. There will be a stitch pattern in this pillow, which means you will be knitting and purling across the row, but it will all be written out so just be careful to count stitches and keep track of which row you are knitting. Also, when directions are written in parentheses, such as (p1, k1), it means to repeat that stitch pattern as many times as the directions immediately after the parentheses dictate, or to the end of the row.

Front

Cast on 61 stitches. Work in seed stitch as follows: k1, (p1, k1) to end of row. Repeat this row until piece measures 1" (2.5 cm). *Next row:* Establish Block Pattern 1 as follows: k1, (p1, k1) twice, place marker, k17, place marker, k1, (p1, k1) 8 times, place marker, k17, place marker, k1, (p1, k1) twice.

Continue in pattern as follows:

Row 1: (wrong side) K1, (p1, k1) to marker; slip marker; purl to next marker; slip marker; k1, (p1, k1) to next marker; slip marker; purl to next marker; slip marker; k1, (p1, k1) to end.

Row 2: K1, (p1, k1) to marker; slip marker; knit to next marker; slip marker; k1, (p1, k1) to next marker; slip marker; knit to next marker; slip marker; k1, (p1, k1) to end.

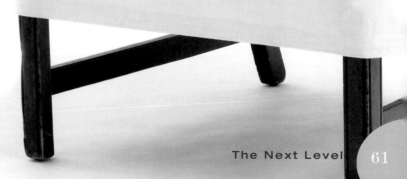

Repeat Rows 1 and 2 until blocks are square—3½" (9 cm) and about 25 rows, if your gauge is the same as ours. Notice whether your last row was a Row 1 or a Row 2.

Change to Block Pattern 2, beginning with Row 1 (if you ended Pattern 1 with Row 2), or beginning with Row 2 (if you ended Pattern 1 with Row 1):

Row 1: (wrong side) K1, (p1, k1) to first marker; slip marker; p1, (k1, p1) to next marker; slip marker; purl to next marker; slip marker; p1, (k1, p1) to next marker; slip marker; k1, (p1, k1) to end.

Row 2: K1, (p1, k1) to first marker; slip marker; p1, (k1, p1) to next marker; slip marker; knit to next marker; slip marker; p1, (k1, p1) to next marker; slip marker; k1, (p1, k1) to end.

Repeat Rows 1 and 2 until blocks are square—again, 3½" (9 cm) and about 25 rows, if your gauge is the same as ours. Notice whether your last row was Row 1 or Row 2.

Work the third row of blocks by following Block Pattern 1 (beginning with whichever row comes next for you). When the blocks in the last row are square, remove all the markers.

Work in seed stitch across all stitches for 1" (2.5 cm).

Bind off all stitches.

Back

Work as for front, but beginning and ending with Block Pattern 2 so that Block Pattern 1 is in the middle.

Finishing

Weave in the loose yarn ends with a tapestry needle on the wrong side of the work. Block pieces to shape, if necessary. With right sides facing you, and with yarn threaded on a tapestry needle, sew front to back along three sides using a whipstitch. The seam is on the right side where it is both visible and decorative so work carefully.

Insert pillow form. Sew fourth side.

Stop Sign Baby Blanket

Your little one will enjoy sweet dreams with this baby blanket in the crib. Knitted in the shape of a stop sign, this soft machine-washable blanket offers you the opportunity to master the art of increasing and decreasing. In no time at all, you'll be wrapping up what will surely be the hit of the baby shower.

Finished Size
36" (91.5 cm) by 36" (91.5 cm) at widest points.

Materials
Yarn: Blanket: CYCA classification: 4 Medium; 1,100 yards (1,005 meters). Letters: CYCA classification: 3 Light; about 246 yards (225 meters).

Shown here: Blanket: Cascade 220 Superwash (100% Superwash wool; 220 yards [201 meters]/100 grams), #808 red (A), 5 skeins. Letters: Rowan Wool Cotton (50% merino wool, 50% cotton; 123 yards [113 meters]/50 grams): #900 antique (B), 2 skeins.

Needles: Size 7 (4.5 mm) 24" (60 cm) circular needle. Adjust needle size if necessary to obtain the correct gauge.

Notions: Tapestry needle; measuring tape; straight pins; stitch holder; size G/6 (4 mm) crochet hook.

Gauge
Blanket: 18 stitches = 4" (10 cm) in garter stitch. Letters: 5½ stitches = 1" (2.5 cm) in garter stitch.

Design
Grace Anna Robbins

Need to know
Cast on (page 18)
Knit stitch (page 20)
Purl stitch (page 22)
Bind off (page 26)
Join a new ball (page 27)
Weave in ends (page 27)
Whipstitch (page 43)
Place stitches on holder (page 50)
Backward loop cast-on (page 52)
Increases (page 52)
Decreases (page 54)

Note

Wash the blanket separately before sewing on the letters to prevent blanket color from bleeding on the letter color.

Blanket

With the blanket yarn and larger circular needles, cast on 54 stitches.

Increase row: Knit into the front and back of the same stitch, knit to the end of the row—55 stitches.

Repeat the increase row every row until there are 162 stitches (108 rows total; 54 garter ridges).

Knit 108 rows even (without increases or decreases) in garter stitch.

Decrease row: Knit 1, knit 2 stitches together, knit to the end of the row—161 stitches remain.

Repeat the decrease row every row until 54 stitches remain.

Bind off all stitches.

Weave in the loose yarn ends with a tapestry needle.

Working Back and Forth on Circular Needles

This blanket is worked back and forth and uses a circular needle to accommodate the number of stitches. To do this, simply cast the stitches onto a circular needle as if it were a single straight needle (ignore the other needle tip). Do not join the stitches into a round, but instead, hold the needle tip containing the stitches in your left hand, use your right hand to pick up the other needle tip as if it were a separate straight needle, and use it to knit back across the row of cast-on stitches. Then turn the work around and use the empty needle tip to knit the stitches off the full tip. It's that easy. You work back and forth in rows just as if you were using two really long straight needles, and because the two needle tips are connected by the plastic (or metal) cable, you can never lose just one of them!

Letters

Review binding off mid-row, page 42, before making letters.

The letter S

Cast on 5 stitches. Knit 10 rows. Cut yarn leaving a 6" (15-cm) tail to weave in later. Place stitches on a stitch holder. Cast on 15 stitches. Work the increase row used for the blanket until there are 25 stitches.

Next row: Knit 5 stitches, bind off 15 stitches, knit 5 stitches (this includes the stitch already on the right needle after the bind-off). Now you will work each side separately. On the side with the yarn attached, knit 10 rows, then bind off these 5 stitches. Attach the yarn to the second side at the bind-off edge and work those 5 stitches for 10 rows. Alternate one increase row with one decrease row 17 times—34 rows total. Work 10 rows even (without increasing or decreasing). Knit 5 stitches, use the backward loop method to cast on 15 stitches, knit 5 stitches from holder—25 stitches. Work the decrease row until 15 stitches remain. Bind off all stitches. Weave in the yarn ends with a tapestry needle.

The letter T

(begin at top) Cast on 25 stitches. Knit 10 rows. Bind off 10 stitches at the beginning of the next 2 rows—5 stitches remain. Knit 48 rows. Bind off all stitches. Weave in the yarn ends with a tapestry needle.

The letter O

Cast on 15 stitches. Work increase row until there are 25 stitches. *Next row:* Knit 5 stitches, bind off 15 stitches, knit 5 stitches. Working each side separately, work 38 rows each. Knit 5 stitches (from one side), use the backward loop method to cast on 15 stitches (for the middle), knit 5 stitches (the other side)—25 stitches. Work the decrease row until 15 stitches remain. Bind off all stitches. Weave in the yarn ends with a tapestry needle.

The letter P

(begin at top) Cast on 20 stitches. Work increase row every other row (along one side only) until there are 25 stitches. *Next row:* Knit 5 stitches, bind off 15 stitches, knit 5 stitches. Working each side separately, work 16 rows each. Knit 5 stitches (from one side), use the backward loop method to cast on 15 stitches (for the middle), knit 5 stitches (the other side)—25 stitches. Work the decrease row every other row (same side as increases were made) until 20 stitches remain. Beginning on the same side the decreases were made (if you find yourself on the opposite side from the decreased edge, knit 1 more row before beginning the bind-off row), bind off 15 stitches, knit to end— 5 stitches remain. Knit 22 rows even. Bind off all stitches. Weave in the yarn ends with a tapestry needle.

Border

With crochet hook and white yarn, work a crochet chain stitch border (see page 113) around the perimeter of the blanket about ½" (1.3 cm) in from the edge.

Finishing

Center the letters and position them with straight pins. Using the letter yarn threaded on a tapestry needle, securely sew the letters onto the blanket using a whipstitch, and making sure the stitches do not penetrate through to the wrong side of the work. Weave in loose yarn tails between the blanket and the letters.

Feed Bag

Design

Lisa R. Myers

Need to know

Cast on (page 18)

Knit stitch (page 20)

Purl stitch (page 22)

Bind off (page 26)

Join a new ball (page 27)

Weave in ends (page 27)

Seaming (page 29)

Whipstitch (page 43)

Place markers (page 49)

Slip stitch (page 50)

Backward loop cast-on (52)

Knitting in the round (page 57)

Tired of carrying your lunch in a plain old bag or the bottom of your briefcase? Give new meaning to "brown-bagging" it with this stylish bag. Knit with sturdy linen yarn, this versatile bag is surprisingly easy to knit up and can also double as a handbag.

Finished Size

6¾" (17 cm) wide by 9" (23 cm) tall by 3¼" (8.5 cm) deep.

Materials

Yarn: CYCA classification: 3 Light; about 380 yards (347.5 meters).

Shown here: Louet Euroflax Geneva (100% linen; 190 yards [173 meters]/100 grams): #18 sandalwood, 2 skeins.

Needles: Size 5 (3.75 mm) 16" (40 cm) circular needle. Adjust needle size if necessary to obtain the correct gauge.

Notions: Four ⅞" (2.2-cm) buttons; four ⅝" (1.5-cm) backing buttons; stitch markers, three of one color and one of another; tapestry needle.

Gauge

22 stitches and 40 rows = 4" (10 cm) in slip-stitch pattern.

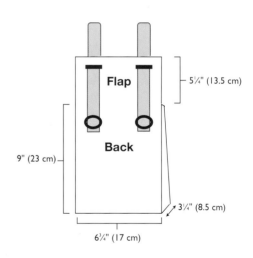

Body

Note: Slip stitches purlwise, unless instructed otherwise.

Cast on 112 stitches. Join for working in the round, being careful not to twist the stitches, and place the unique-colored marker to indicate beginning of round.

Set-up round: Knit 37 (for back and flap), place marker, knit 19 (for side panel), place marker, knit 37 (for front), place marker, knit 19 (for other side panel).

Round 1: *Slip marker, slip next 2 stitches with yarn in back, (purl 5, slip 1 stitch with yarn in back) 5 times, purl 5; slip marker, slip next 2 stitches with yarn in back, (purl 5, slip 1 stitch with yarn in back) 2 times, purl 5; repeat from * to end of round.

Round 2: Knit, slipping markers from left to right needle as you meet them.

Repeat Rounds 1 and 2 until piece measures 9" (23 cm), ending with Round 2.

Shape flap

Slip 2 stitches with yarn in back, (purl 5, slip 1 stitch with yarn in back) 5 times, purl 5; remove marker, slip 2 stitches with yarn in back, re-place marker (these last 39 stitches will serve as the flap in upcoming rows), knit the next 73 stitches and bind them off as you go, thus ending at the beginning of the round (use the first stitch of the next round to complete binding off the last stitch). Remove all stitch markers as you bind off. Now continue on the 39 remaining stitches for the flap, working back and forth in rows as follows:

Row 1: Knit.

Row 2: Slip 2 stitches with yarn in front, (knit 5, slip 1 stitch with yarn in front) 6 times, slip last stitch with yarn in front.

Repeat Rows 1 and 2 until flap measures 4" (10 cm), ending with Row 2. Make buttonholes in next row as follows:

Buttonhole row: Knit 8, bind off next 5 stitches, knit 13 (including the stitch already on the right needle from the bind-off), bind off next 5 stitches, knit to end of row (you should have 8 stitches on the right needle after the last bind-off).

Next row: Slip 2 stitches with yarn in front, knit 5, purl 1, use the backward loop method to cast on 5 stitches to complete the buttonhole, purl 1, knit 5, slip 1 stitch with yarn in front, knit 5, purl 1, cast on 5 stitches same as before, purl 1, knit 5, slip 2 stitches with yarn in front. *Note:* On the next row, work into the back loops of the 10 cast-on stitches (over the buttonholes). Knit the rest of the row as usual. On subsequent rows, work all stitches as usual following the pattern.

Beginning with Row 1, work 1" (2.5 cm) more in Slip Stitch Pattern, ending with Row 2.

Bind off all stitches knitwise.

Base

Leaving a particularly long tail (say, an extra 36" [91.5 cm]) to assist with assembly later, cast on 36 stitches. Knit every row until piece measures 3" (7.5 cm). Bind off all stitches. Leave an extra 36" (91.5 cm) or so when cutting yarn after bind-off.

Straps (make 2)

Leaving an extra-long tail (say, an extra 15" [38 cm]), cast on 5 stitches. Knit every row until piece measures 18" (45.5 cm) from cast-on. Bind off all stitches, leaving about 15" (38 cm) for the tail when cutting yarn.

Finishing

Sew base into bottom of bag
Hold wrong sides together and sew with a whipstitch. Weave in the loose yarn ends with a tapestry needle.

Attach straps
On back of bag, pin one strap to the second wide stripe and one to the fifth, 7" (18 cm) up from bottom of bag. Sew straps onto bag with whipstitch around bottom 1" (2.5 cm) of strap. Thread straps through buttonholes on flap and pin each strap to its corresponding stripe, 3¼" (8.5 cm) up from bottom of bag. Whipstitch ends of straps around bottom 1" (2.5 cm). Sew one button onto each end of each strap, using backing button on inside of bag. Depending on the size of the holes in the buttons, you may want to use buttonhole or embroidery thread in the same color as your yarn when attaching the buttons. Weave in remaining yarn ends with a tapestry needle.

Half-Square Triangular Shawl

Knit in a cheery pink, this project riffs on the grandmothery shawl of generations past but makes it surprisingly modern. Why the half square? For those of you who remember symmetry, there is more than one way to divide a square in half. Grab a piece of origami paper. Fold the top left-hand corner across to the bottom right-hand corner. See? Half-square triangle!

Design

Grace Anna Robbins

Need to know

Cast on (page 18)
Knit stitch (page 20)
Purl stitch (page 22)
Bind off (page 26)
Weave in ends (page 27)
Join a new ball (page 27)
Pass slipped stitch over (page 50)
Slip stitch (page 50)
Backward loop cast-on (page 52)
Increases (page 52)
Yarnover (page 53)
Decreases (page 54)
I-cord (page 89)

Finished Size

70" (178 cm) across (base of triangle) by 35" (89 cm) long (neck to point), after blocking.

Materials

Yarn: CYCA classification: 1 Super Fine; about 680 yards (620 meters).

Shown here: Koigu KPM (100% merino wool; 170 yards [155 meters]/50 grams): #P1175, 4 skeins.

Needles: Size 8 (5 mm) circular needles at least 24" (60 cm) long (you'll be using them like straight needles).

Notions: Stitch markers; tapestry needle; long straight sewing pins with large colored heads (or T-pins), to use when blocking.

Gauge

16 stitches = 4" (10 cm) over stockinette stitch.

Abbreviations

k1f&b: Knit into front and back loop of same stitch (page 52)

yo: Yarnover (page 53)

k2tog: Knit two stitches together (page 54)

ssk: Slip, slip, knit decrease (page 55)

Shawl

Cast on 2 stitches.

Set up the pattern

Set-up Row 1: K1f&b in each stitch—4 stitches.

Set-up Row 2: K1f&b, k1f&b, yarnover, k1f&b, k1f&b—9 stitches.

Set-up Row 3: Knit 4, yarnover, knit 1, place a marker *in* the stitch you just knit, yarnover, knit 4—11 stitches.

What have you set up?

This shawl is knit from the center of the neck outward, increasing four times every other row. The first four and the last four stitches of every row are always knitted, which creates an edging, border, or selvedge. Whatever you call it, these four stitches prevent the work at the beginning and end of the row from curling. On the right-side rows, you'll knit the border stitches, yarnover (a form of increase abbreviated as "yo"), knit to the center stitch, yarnover, knit the center stitch, yarnover, knit to the border stitches, yarnover, knit the border stitches. So you have worked one row, increasing four times, one increase at each edge and two increases in the middle.

Row 4: Knit 4, purl to last 4 stitches, knit 4.

Row 5: Knit 4, yo, knit 1, yo, knit 1 (the center marked stitch), yo, knit 1, yo, knit 4—15 stitches.

Row 6: Knit 4, purl to the last 4 stitches, knit 4.

Row 7: Knit 4, yo, knit 3, yo, knit 1 (the center marked stitch), yo, knit 3, yo, knit 4—19 stitches.

Row 8: Knit 4, purl to the last 4 stitches, knit 4.

The pattern row

Row 9: Knit 4, yo, knit 1, *(yo, k2tog); repeat from * to center marked stitch, yo, knit 1, yo, *(k2tog, yo); repeat from * to last 5 stitches, knit 1, yo, knit 4—23 stitches.

Say what?

The first and the last 4 stitches remain knit stitches. The center sequence remains "yarnover, k1, yarnover" but now you are increasing (yarnover) and decreasing (k2tog) everywhere else. Why the extra k1 at the beginning and end of the row right before the borders? Two reasons. First, when there are two yarnovers next to each other they create a larger hole that needs special treatment on the following row or round so usually they are separated by one or more knit stitches (like the center increase "yarnover, k1, yarnover"). Second, there needs to be 4 extra yarnovers with no corresponding decreases so that you maintain the half square triangle increase rate (see box below) so knit 1 instead of k2tog.

What are those asterisks doing there?

The instructions within the parentheses that are preceded by an asterisk are repeated as instructed.

About Those Increases

Fold the top left-hand corner of a piece of origami paper across the bottom right-hand corner. Now fold that same piece of paper in half diagonal again, but the other way so the top right-hand corner is crossing over to the bottom left-hand corner. Now you have four quadrants.

Incidentally, for those of you who missed geometry, each of these quadrants is also a half-square triangle. Every isosceles triangle (a triangle with two sides that are the same length) that also has a 90-degree angle will always be a half-square triangle. When you divided the square in half again, you bisected (to divide into two pieces usually equal) the hypotenuse (the long side that is different from the other two), which had been a straight line. How many degrees are in a straight line? 180. What is half of 180? 90! More half-square triangles! You may have guessed that this could go on and on forever.

If you were knitting a square and increasing it outwards from the middle, you would increase twice at each of these fold lines every other row or round. So two new stitches at four points is eight new stitches every other row or round. The increase method in this pattern is ". . ., yarnover, knit 1, yarnover, . . ."

But you are making a *half*-square triangle, so you only need half (or 4) of these increases. When you folded the paper the first time, how many angles were changed and how many were omitted and how many remained unchanged? Two angles changed from 90 degrees to half that, or 45; one angle was omitted entirely, and one remained unchanged. So instead of ". . . yarnover, knit 1, yarnover, . . . " four times, you need only one yarnover at two points (the outside edges) and one unchanged sequence at the center of the triangle. Four increases at three points.

The rest of the shawl

Work the next 6 rows (the 5 stockinette stitch rows and the 1 eyelet row) as follows:

Row 10: Knit 4, purl to the last 4 stitches, knit 4.

Row 11: Knit 4, yo, knit to the center marked stitch, yo, knit 1, yo, knit to the last 4 stitches, yo, knit 4—4 stitches have been increased; 27 stitches total.

Row 12: Knit 4, purl to the last 4 stitches, knit 4.

Row 13: Knit 4, yo, knit to the center marked stitch, yo, knit 1, yo, knit to the last 4 stitches, yo, knit 4—4 stitches have been increased; 31 stitches total.

Row 14: Knit 4, purl to the last 4 stitches, knit 4.

Row 15: Knit 4, yo, knit 1, *(yo, k2tog), repeat from * to the center marked stitch, yo, knit 1, yo, *(k2tog, yo), repeat from * to last 5 stitches, knit 1, yo, knit 4—4 stitches have been increased—35 stitches.

Work the last 6 rows a total of 24 times (144 rows total); the shawl ends with a total of 311 stitches (this number includes the 23 stitches from the previous rows).

The marked stitch

As your work progresses, the marker you placed will grow farther and farther away. You should either move the marker up after every couple of rows (for instance after every pattern row), or place a new marker into the work every couple of rows (or as you need it).

Tip: Count the stitches after every increase row; if you have too many or too few, you may have dropped a yarnover, forgot to make a yarnover, or didn't work the decrease (these are the usual culprits in openwork patterns). Look at the stitches very carefully and you may spot the problem and not have to remove the entire row to correct it.

Almost done

The last row will be the eyelet row (right side of work), and after completing that row you'll have 311 stitches.

The shawl at this point will use about 3½ balls of the yarn listed above, if your work is on gauge. We'll use the remainder of the yarn to finish the edges. Instead of the usual bind off, we're going to finish the shawl with an I-cord bind-off. That means we'll be knitting an I-cord and attaching it to the live stitches at the same time.

The I-cord bind-off

With the working yarn still attached, turn the work to the wrong side. Using the backward loop method, cast on 3 stitches onto the left needle (circular) holding the shawl stitches; these 3 stitches are the I-cord stitches and will sit on the needle in front of the shawl stitches. Using a double-pointed needle in the right hand, knit the 3 stitches. Slip them purlwise back onto the left needle in front of the shawl stitches (*Note:* the working yarn will be at the far end of the I-cord stitches, and ahead of the shawl stitches.)

*Pull the yarn across the back of the I-cord stitches to the front of the left needle tip, then using the double-pointed needle in your right hand, knit 2 of the three I-cord stitches, then work the ssk decrease as follows: slip the third I-cord stitch knitwise onto the double-pointed needle, slip the next stitch (this will be a shawl stitch) knitwise onto the double-pointed needle, insert the left needle tip through the fronts of both slipped stitches and knit them together in this position—3 stitches (I-cord) remain on the double-pointed needle. Slip these 3 stitches back onto the circular needle in front of the shawl stitches and repeat from * until all the shawl stitches are worked into the I-cord bind-off. When the last shawl stitch is worked into the I-cord bind-off, slip the remaining 3 stitches back to the left needle, slip 1, ssk, pass slipped stitch over (psso). Cut yarn leaving 4" (10-cm) tail, thread through remaining stitch and pull tail to fasten off. Thread tail on tapestry needle and weave tail through center of I-cord.

Finishing

The knitting is finished and the shawl probably resembles a crumpled dishrag. This section is where we turn it into a swan. Weave in the yarn ends very loosely. Do not cut the tails yet. Soak your shawl in lukewarm soapy water (mild dishwashing liquid is okay) for about 10–15 minutes. Drain the water without removing the shawl from the sink. Then gently squeeze (don't wring) the shawl several times to remove excess water, place the shawl on a drain board. When removing the shawl from the sink, scoop it up using both hands. Avoid picking it up by an edge and stretching it prematurely. Fill the sink with lukewarm water, place the shawl in the sink again and rinse carefully. You may have to repeat the rinse process several times to remove all the soapiness . . . drain the sink, squeeze excess water from the shawl, remove shawl from sink, fill sink with fresh rinse water, insert the shawl into the rinse water. At no time during this process should you allow water to pour directly onto the shawl!

If you used wool yarn for your shawl, as we did, pour a small amount of white vinegar into the next-to-last-rinse water (a tad less than ⅛ cup [30 ml] vinegar per average kitchen sink filled with water). *Note:* Use *white* vinegar only, no balsamic, raspberry, or other gourmet vinegars, keep those for your salads. The shawl will smell like vinegar when you're through, but it's temporary. The vinegar removes any soapy residue, does not harm wool, and will help soften the fiber. Gently squeeze out the excess rinse water.

Roll up the entire shawl in a large oversize bath towel. Check to make sure no shawl pieces are hanging out of the roll. Place the towel on the floor and step on it (with full weight) several times, moving your feet so all areas are stepped on several times. Remove the shawl from the towel and shake it a couple of times. Lay out the shawl onto a large clean flat surface. A spare bedroom floor, or spare bed are good places for blocking shawls. Remember, once you have the shawl stretched and pinned, it shouldn't be moved until dry. Spread a flat bedsheet over the flat surface and place your shawl on top of the sheet. Gently pat and stretch into a triangular shape. When you have the shawl fully stretched out, both width and length, measure carefully to make sure the shawl matches the measurements given. If not, stretch, smooth, and pat some more. Using rustproof pins, pin the shawl around the three edges into its triangular shape. Then walk away and close the door! Let the shawl air-dry completely before moving. When dry, remove all pins; check to see if the yarn ends you wove in need adjusting. Trim ends.

Rock and Roll Brim Hat

Design
Grace Anna Robbins

Need to know
Cast on (page 18)
Knit stitch (page 20)
Join a new ball (page 27)
Weave in ends (page 27)
Place markers (page 49)
Decreases (page 54)
Knitting in the round (page 57)

This super-simple hat is a great choice for men and women alike, and is sure to be the everyday "goes with everything" go-to hat. We knit it with super-soft Rowan Cashsoft DK yarn for added yumminess. It knits up fast, so you might find yourself making one for friends and family as cold weather approaches. They'll thank you for it. Oh, and since it has a loose fit, you'll never have to fear the dreaded hat head.

Finished Size
22" (56 cm) circumference and 9" (23 cm) long with edge unrolled. About 7" (18 cm) long with edge rolled upward.

Materials
Yarn: CYCA classification: 3 Light; about 286 yards (260 meters).
Shown here: Rowan Cashsoft DK (57% extra fine merino wool, 33% microfiber, 10% cashmere; 143 yards [130 meters]/50 grams): #513 poison, 2 skeins.

Needles: Size 6 (4 mm) 16" (40 cm) circular needle; 1 set (4 or 5) Size 6 (4 mm) double-pointed needles. Adjust needle size if necessary to obtain the correct gauge.
Notions: 8 stitch markers (one should be a different color); measuring tape or ruler; tapestry needle.

Gauge
22 stitches = 4" (10 cm) in stockinette stitch worked in the round.

Brim

Cast on 120 stitches on the circular needle. Place different-colored marker and join for working in the round, being careful not to twist the stitches.

Knit every stitch of every round until hat measures 7" (18 cm) from the cast-on edge (the cast-on edge curls upward, so carefully smooth it straight without stretching the length when measuring).

Crown

Next round: Slip marker, *(knit 15 stitches, place marker); repeat from * to end of round (8 markers in place).

Decrease rounds: *(Knit to 2 stitches before marker, knit 2 together); repeat from * every round until 8 stitches remain (14 decrease rounds), changing to double-pointed needles when there are too few stitches to fit on the circular needle.

Cut yarn, leaving a 10" (25.5-cm) tail. Thread tail onto tapestry needle, pull it through the remaining stitches, and secure on the wrong side.

Finishing

Weave in the loose yarn ends with a tapestry needle.

Add a flower embellishment (page 120), if desired.

Cable Cap

Design

Grace Anna Robbins

A great introduction to the marvel of cabling, our cap fits over the ears like a traditional watch cap.

Need to know

Cast on (page 18)

Knit stitch (page 20)

Purl stitch (page 22)

Weave in ends (page 27)

Place markers (page 49)

Slip stitch (page 50)

Decreases (page 54)

Cables (page 55)

Knitting in the round (page 57)

Finished Size

20" circumference, slightly stretched and about 10" (25.5 cm) long.

Materials

Yarn: CYCA classification: 4 Medium; about 37 yards (126 meters).

Shown here: Manos del Uruguay (100% wool; 137 yards [126 meters]/100 grams): #69 hibiscus, 1 skein.

Needles: Size 9 (5.5 mm) 16" (40-cm) circular needle; set of size 9 (5.5 mm) double-pointed needles. Adjust needle size if necessary to obtain the correct gauge.

Notions: Stitch marker; cable needle; measuring tape; tapestry needle.

Gauge

16 stitches = 4" (10 cm) in stockinette stitch.

Abbreviations

4/4RC cable (4-stitch right-cross cable): Slip 4 stitches onto the cable needle and hold in back of the work. Knit 4 stitches from the left knitting needle and then knit the 4 stitches from the cable needle, thus creating a twist in your row of knitting.

Cable decrease: Slip the specified number of stitches onto a cable needle and hold in back of work. *(Knit 1 stitch from the left needle, together with 1 stitch from the cable needle); repeat from * until all of the stitches have been worked from the cable needle.

In other words: Bring the cable needle toward the left needle so it sits behind of and parallel to the left needle. The first stitch on the cable needle will be aligned with the first stitch on the left needle. *Working the stitches in order of their presentation, slip the right needle into both the first stitch on the left needle and the first stitch on the cable needle, and knit the two stitches together; repeat from * until all stitches from the cable needle are worked together with those on the left needle.

Brim

Cast on 80 stitches onto circular needle. Join for working in the round, being careful not to twist the stitches, and place a stitch marker to indicate the beginning of the round.

*(Knit 3, purl 2); repeat from * to end of round.

Repeat this round until piece measures 1" (2.5 cm) from cast-on.

Pattern set-up rounds: *(Knit 8, purl 2); repeat from * around for 3 rounds.

Cable pattern

Round 1: *(4/4 RC, purl 2, knit 8, purl 2); repeat from * to end of round.

Rounds 2–7: *(Knit 8, purl 2); repeat from * to end of round.

Round 8: *(Knit 8, purl 2, 4/4 RC, purl 2); repeat from * to end of round.

Rounds 9–15: *(Knit 8, purl 2); repeat from * to end of round.

Repeat Rounds 1–15 until the hat measures about 6" (15 cm) long from cast-on edge.

Crown

Round 1: *(Cable decrease 4, purl 2, knit 8, purl 2); repeat from * to end of round—64 stitches remain.

Rounds 2–8: *(Knit 4, purl 2, knit 8, purl 2); repeat from * to end of round.

Round 9: *(Knit 4, purl 2, cable decrease 4, purl 2); repeat from * to end of round—48 stitches remain.

Rounds 10 and 11: *(Knit 4, purl 2); repeat from * to end of round.

Round 12: *(Cable decrease 2, purl 2, knit 4); repeat from * to end of round—40 stitches remain.

Rounds 13 and 14: *(Knit 2, purl 2, knit 4, purl 2); repeat from * to end of round. Change to double-pointed needles.

Round 15: *(Knit 2, purl 2, cable decrease 2, purl 2); repeat from * to end of round—32 stitches remain.

Round 16: *(Knit 2, purl 2); repeat from * to end of round.

Round 17: *(Slip 1 stitch purlwise, knit 1, purl 2 together); repeat from * to end of round—24 stitches remain.

Round 18: *(Knit 1, knit 2 together—one of these will be a knit stitch; the other will be purl stitch); repeat from * to end of round—16 stitches remain.

Round 19: Knit 2 together to end of round—8 stitches remain.

Finishing

Cut yarn, leaving a 10" (25.5-cm) tail. Thread tail onto tapestry needle, pull it through the remaining stitches, and secure on the wrong side. Weave in the loose yarn ends with a tapestry needle.

If you want, top your hat with a full and fluffy pom-pom (page 112).

Ballet School Dropout Leg Warmers

Design

Courtney Kelley

Need to know

Cast on (page 18)

Knit stitch (page 20)

Purl stitch (page 22)

Ribbing (page 25)

Bind off (page 26)

Weave in ends (page 27)

Place markers (page 49)

Knitting in the round (page 57)

What a feeling! Knit in the round, these ribbed leg warmers will warm your legs and make you want to bust out dancing (or at least do a bit of stretching). This is a great variation of basic skills: knitting, purling, and knitting in the round. That's pretty much it, so experiment. You can always use another pair of leg warmers—and trust us, they've come a long way from those neon pink ones you owned in 1984.

Finished Size

About 10" (25.5 cm) circumference with ribbing relaxed, and 16" (40.5 cm) long. Will stretch to 18" (45.5) circumference.

Materials

Yarn: CYCA classification: 4 Medium; about 308 yards (280 meters).

Shown here: Rowan Kid Classic (70% lambswool, 26% kid mohair, 4% nylon; 154 yards [140 meters]/50 grams): #835 royal, 2 skeins.

Needles: Size 8 (5 mm): set of 5 double-pointed needles or 12" (30.5-cm) circular needle. Adjust needle size if necessary to obtain the correct gauge.

Notions: Measuring tape; tapestry needle, stitch marker.

Gauge

18 stitches = 4" (10 cm) in stockinette stitch.

Tip: It is helpful to cast on and bind off with a needle that is at least one or two sizes larger than the one used to get the recommended gauge. This will ensure that the leg warmers will pull on and off easily.

Leg warmer (make 2)

Cast on 64 stitches. If using double-pointed needles, divide stitches evenly onto 4 double-pointed needles (16 stitches on each needle). Join for working in the round, being careful not to twist the stitches, and place a marker to indicate the beginning of the round. Work in knit 2, purl 2 rib until piece measures 16" (40.5 cm) from cast-on, or desired length. Bind off all stitches.

Finishing

Weave in the loose yarn ends with a tapestry needle.

The Garment District

Legend has it that if you surprise your boyfriend with a knitted gift—even if it's just an innocuous scarf—you will doom the relationship.

You design your own sweater when you:

a) choose a yarn.

b) shape it for a custom fit.

c) embellish it.

d) all of the above.

According to knitting lore, for whom should you never knit something?

a) Mother.

b) Boss.

c) Spouse.

d) Boyfriend.

The key to a good fit is:

a) checking gauge.

b) measuring your knitting frequently.

c) taking accurate measurements of the intended wearer.

d) all of the above.

A stitch chart should always be read:

a) from top to bottom.

b) from bottom to top.

c) from right to left.

d) starting with the first empty square.

When knitting a sweater, it is not necessary to measure a person's:

a) foot.

b) arm.

c) waist.

d) chest.

Answers: d, d, d, b, a.

The time is at hand to knit a full-fledged garment! At this point, you have all the skills necessary to create a gorgeous sweater for yourself or a loved one (but never a boyfriend! More on that below). You can cast on, knit, and purl, all the while reading a pattern. You've most likely increased, decreased, and sewn a few pieces together. Coupled with passion for your craft, you possess all the skills necessary to knit the sweater of your dreams.

One of the many beauties of knitting a sweater is that you can customize everything about it: the style, the fit, the color, the fiber. You can ensure that the garment is both flattering and comfortable, not to mention praiseworthy. In our Stunningly Simple Sweater Studio (page 100), we give you two very different sweaters based on the same basic pattern. Sounds hard? It's not! Just remember to take one piece of the pattern at a time and before long, you'll be seaming together the last two pieces. So let's get started knitting the sweater of your dreams!

The Boyfriend Curse

It is worth mentioning that you should never, ever knit something for a boyfriend. It's bound to end badly (the relationship, not the garment). Legend has it that if you surprise your boyfriend with a knitted gift—even if it's just an innocuous scarf—you will doom the relationship. The reasons could be one or many. Perhaps he will feel that you don't know him at all, or you would *never* have made him a scarf in the colors of his rival high school. Or used an itchy wool when you *know* he only wears cotton or cashmere. Or made him a hat when he *never* wears hats. Maybe the gift of your time and care freaks him out. Maybe he can project the two of you sitting in rocking chairs in your old age, you knitting and him wishing he had learned. Maybe it's just bad luck, pure and simple. Whatever the case, if you have a superstitious bone in your body, make sure your relationship is rock solid before you decide to surprise him with merino socks.

That said, you might choose to poo-poo superstition or ignore those who crashed and burned before you. Brave soul. If you must absolutely knit something for your significant other, ask some questions and get the lay of the land before knitting something that's too bright, too boring, or too scratchy. Pay attention to what garment he always reaches for, the colors he (not you) likes, and his overall style. Heeding these clues will improve your odds of knitting an item he cherishes, not one that is stuffed into a bottom drawer and never sees the light of day.

MEASURING UP

Don't assume someone has a "normal" frame, whatever you think that is. You need more specifics than that.

Measuring Tape

Up to now, taking measurements of the intended wearer has been relatively easy. Most scarves will "fit" anyone, unless the person is very tall or very short, in which case you just knit more or less to make it longer or shorter. But with sweaters, vests, tops of all kinds, skirts, and the like, it is extremely important that you not only knit to gauge but that you know the body measurements you are knitting for.

First of all, don't assume someone has a "normal" frame, whatever you think that is. You need more specifics than that. While you might think your mom is pretty much the same size as you, she might have a smaller bust or broader shoulders, so you need to knit accordingly. If you want a garment to fit properly, it's extremely challenging to knit something as a surprise. But you can still wow someone with an unexpected knitted gift even if you measure them. Just don't tell them what you're knitting or when.

It's probably a good idea to measure all of your loved ones and keep a log. But keep in mind that while height may not change much (unless you're knitting for a child), other parts of a body or frame are subject to change. Chest, bust, and waist size all can fluctuate so take a fresh set of measurements with each new project, especially if there is little **ease** in the garment you are planning to knit.

Speaking of ease, don't make assumptions about shape and fit, either. You may think your best friend is tall and willowy and would look fantastic in an easy breezy tunic. However, she may feel that her large bust size makes large, roomy sweaters look as if she's wearing a tent. She may prefer fitted, shapely cardigans. So pay attention to the clothes she wears and ask her about her clothing preferences.

So how do you actually take measurements, and what do you need to measure? Excellent questions!

First of all, you'll need a **tape measure** (perhaps I'm stating the obvious). For a sweater, the key measurements to take are the bust/chest width, waist, sleeve length, shoulder width, and overall length. With the tape measure, measure around your torso at the widest part of the bust or chest, around your waist, from shoulder to wrist, from the outside of one shoulder to the other, and from shoulder to waist (or wherever you want the sweater to hit). Alternatively, you can also measure a favorite sweater. Jot these numbers down.

Now, compare them to the measurements listed in the pattern or shown on the schematic. They should come close to one of the measurements listed in the pattern. Patterns include a set of measurements, starting with the smallest, followed by the other sizes in parentheses. Depending on the amount of ease you want, choose a size that is bigger than your body measurements. If you want a close fit, choose the size that most closely matches your body. If you want a roomy sweater, choose one of the larger sizes.

And it's usually relatively easy to customize a pattern if it doesn't look like it will fit quite right. For example, if you suspect the sleeve length will be too short, add a couple of inches to the sleeve length while you are knitting, being careful to take into consideration any stitch pattern or increases. If the sweater pattern calls for a longer length than you'd like, subtract some inches (or centimeters) while you're knitting the front and back pieces (or the body of the sweater if knitting in the round) and do it before you hit the armhole shaping instructions. Taking some time at the outset to plan a few modifications will help to produce a perfect-fitting garment.

Taking some time at the outset to plan a few modifications will help to produce a perfect-fitting garment.

READING PATTERNS

Some patterns resemble an elegant minimalist haiku, assuming the knitter is intuitive and can read between the lines.

When you venture outside this book into the wide world of knitting, you'll find that **patterns** vary in terms of instruction. Some patterns resemble an elegant minimalist haiku, assuming the knitter is intuitive and can read between the lines. Text is minimal and the accompanying schematics and pattern charts look like they require a decoder ring to decipher.

In contrast, some patterns spell everything out and opt for clarity over brevity. You might think it obvious that the latter is always the better method but you might be surprised at how much you already know. For instance, you can easily discern that "St st" is stockinette stitch and that "k" and "p" stand for knit and purl, respectively. This foreign language is becoming second nature and even if it feels awkward at first, learning to speak *all* dialects in the knitting world will allow you to travel with ease through any book, magazine, or individual pattern.

As you've seen in the patterns featured in this book, there are some basic elements that are included with the text: finished size of garment, knitted gauge, a materials list (a recommended yarn and needle size, as well as other "notions" you might need, such as ring markers, tapestry needle, or buttons). Special notes about the pattern, sizing, or abbreviations are listed up front as well. Written directions follow, taking you step by step through the knitting of each piece, ending with instructions for blocking, seaming, and otherwise finishing your garment.

In addition to written instructions, patterns generally include a **schematic,** a line drawing of the garment, both front and back (if it's necessary to see both sides of the garment). Key measurements are included for every size. For instance, sets of numbers might be given for the body length, from waistband to armhole shaping, from waistband to shoulder shaping, and from waistband to neck shaping. The first number denotes the smallest size and is followed by measurements for other sizes in parentheses.

Schematic for Go-To Pullover

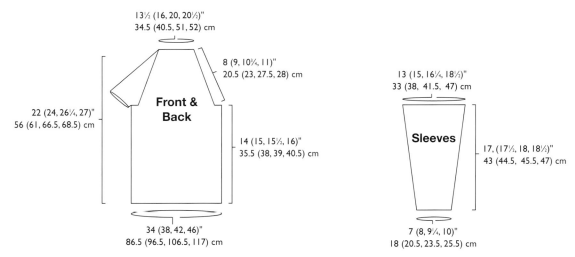

13½ (16, 20, 20½)"
34.5 (40.5, 51, 52) cm

8 (9, 10¾, 11)"
20.5 (23, 27.5, 28) cm

Front & Back

22 (24, 26¼, 27)"
56 (61, 66.5, 68.5) cm

14 (15, 15½, 16)"
35.5 (38, 39, 40.5) cm

34 (38, 42, 46)"
86.5 (96.5, 106.5, 117) cm

13 (15, 16¼, 18½)"
33 (38, 41.5, 47) cm

Sleeves

17, (17½, 18, 18½)"
43 (44.5, 45.5, 47) cm

7 (8, 9¼, 10)"
18 (20.5, 23.5, 25.5) cm

For instance: "14 (15, 15½, 16)" (35.5 [38, 39, 40.5] cm)" indicates that you need to knit 14" (35.5 cm) for the smallest size, 15" (38 cm) for medium, 15½" (39 cm) for large, or 16" (40.5 cm) for the largest size garment for that particular block of knitting.

A stitch pattern or color chart is also featured, if the garment merits it. Read on.

READING A CHART

Always read a chart starting at the bottom.

Deciphering a **chart** takes a little getting used to at first. Resembling a grid or graph paper, each square in a chart represents one stitch. For color work, the chart might be in color and used to denote when you should change yarns to achieve a desired color pattern in your design. Most often, however, there are different symbols in the chart to indicate a different stitch. For example, empty boxes might indicate a knit stitch, solid boxes are for purl stitches, and a diagonal line through three boxes might indicate for you to cable those three stitches. A legend almost always accompanies the chart, so you can easily refer to it for guidance.

Knit on right side; purl on wrong side

On right-side rows, slip 1, knit 2 together, pass slipped stitch over.
On wrong-side rows (purl): purl 2 stitches together, return the decreased
stitch to the left needle, pass the next stitch on the left needle over the
decreased stitch, then return the decreased stitch back to the right needle.

Knit 2 together decrease

Slip, slip, knit decrease

Yarnover

Pattern repeat

Sample chart

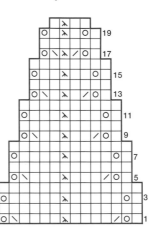

Now, as for what direction you should read a chart. Always read a chart starting at the bottom. So the bottom right box is always the first stitch on the first row after your cast-on row. Charts always show the right side of the knitting. This means that if you are knitting a flat piece on straight needles, then you read from right to left on Row 1, from left to right on Row 2, and so on. If you are knitting in the round, then you knit from right to left on every round.

BUTTONHOLES

By now you won't be surprised to know that, like most things in knitting, there are several ways to create **buttonholes.** An easy way to create a hole for a small button is to knit two together and yarnover right before or after. When knitting the next row, work that yarnover as a stitch and you've created a small gap in your knitting. This is more of a vertical buttonhole, perfect for a small button.

To create a more distinct, larger, and horizontal buttonhole, you'll need to work it in two steps over two rows:

Step 1: On the first row of your buttonhole, bind off a few stitches (two to three, depending on the size of your button) where you want your buttonhole to be (Figure 1). It will seem weird to bind off stitches mid-row, but it works!

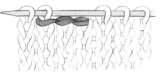

Figure 1. Bind off a few stitches on the first buttonhole row.

Step 2: On the next row, when you get to the bound-off stitches, cast on the same number of stitches you bound off in the previous row (Figure 2). A long-tail cast-on doesn't work real well here. Better to do a super-easy cast-on: If you're working a purl row, keep the yarn in front and twist it to form a backward loop (see page 52). You have a new stitch! Add as many more stitches as you need to match the number of bind-off stitches, then continue the purl row. If you're working a knit row, keep the yarn in back and make the cast-on stitches same as above. You have created a sturdy buttonhole! On the next row, work into the back loops of the cast-on stitches to keep them neat and snug.

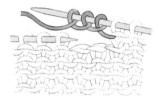

Figure 2. Cast on the same number of stitches on the following row.

I-CORD

I-cord is an often overlooked and underrated technique in knitting that produces a sturdy tube suitable for straps and edgings.

Step 1: Cast on a few stitches (three to five is usually a good number) on a double-pointed needle (in a smaller size than the larger project you've been knitting).

Step 2: Slide the stitches to the other end of the needle (so that the first stitch you cast on is the one closest to the point). This needle now becomes your left-hand needle. The working yarn, however, is coming from the left-most stitch, rather than the first stitch to be worked.

Step 3: Pull the yarn across the back and knit the stitches.

Repeat Steps 2 and 3 until your I-cord is the desired length. The work will become tube-like after several rows. Bind off all of the stitches.

I-cord is worked over a small number of stitches with the same side of the work always facing you.

VARIATIONS ON A THEME:
Lace Capelet and Skirt

This versatile design can be knitted up to create a charming capelet or a sassy skirt. The chevron pattern looks quite elaborate, but once you get the stitch pattern down (don't worry, it only uses techniques and stitches from Chapters 2 and 3), it's a breeze.

We even show you how to knit a pocket incorporating intarsia color work as well. And with handy I-cord, you can create a tie for the capelet or a drawstring waistband for your skirt.

The Capelet

This capelet is a great alternative to a jacket and can be dressed up or down, depending on your mood. And unlike some garments, this will always fit!

Design

Courtney Kelley

Finished Size

34 (45)" (86.5 [114.5] cm) lower edge circumference and 16 (18)" (40.5 [45.5] cm) long, after blocking. To fit 28–34 (36–40)" (71–86.5 [91.5–101.5] cm) chest. Capelet shown in size small.

Materials

Yarn: CYCA classification: 4 Medium; about 392 (588) yards (360 [540] meters).

Shown here: Rowan All-Seasons Cotton (60% cotton, 40% acrylic; 98 yards [90 meters]/ 50 grams): #211 blackcurrant, 4 (6) skeins.

Needles: Size 8 (5 mm) straight needles and set of 2 double-pointed needles. Adjust needle size if necessary to obtain the correct gauge.

Notions: Measuring tape; tapestry needle; long sewing pins with colored heads, or T-pins.

Gauge

16-stitch repeat = 3" (7.5 cm); 4-stitch repeat = 1" (2.5 cm).

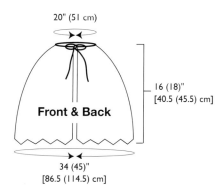

20" (51 cm)

Front & Back

16 (18)" [40.5 (45.5) cm]

34 (45)" [86.5 (114.5) cm]

Notes

Instructions are given for two sizes, small and medium, which contain 11 and 15 panels, respectively. The number of stitches or length measurement for size small is given first, with that for size medium immediately following in parentheses. When only one number appears, it applies to both sizes.

You may want to place a marker before the first stitch of every pattern repeat to help you keep your place.

Abbreviations

psso: Pass slipped stitch over (page 50)
sl 1: Slip 1 stitch knitwise (page 50)
yo: Yarnover (page 53)
k2tog: Knit 2 stitches together (page 54)
ssk: Slip, slip, knit decrease (page 55)

2-Row Stitch Pattern:

Row 1: (right side) *Knit 1, yo, knit 6, sl 1, k2tog, psso, knit 6, yo; repeat from *, end knit 1.

Row 2: (wrong side) Purl.

Repeat Rows 1 and 2 for pattern.

Capelet

Cast on 177 (241) stitches—16 sts for each panel plus 1 extra stitch to balance the center front edge.

Work the 2-row pattern stitch until piece measures 12 (14)" (30.5 [35.5] cm) from beginning.

Note: When the shoulder shaping begins, no extra shaping decreases are made in the first and last panels. Special decrease shaping occurs in the other 9 (13) panels only.

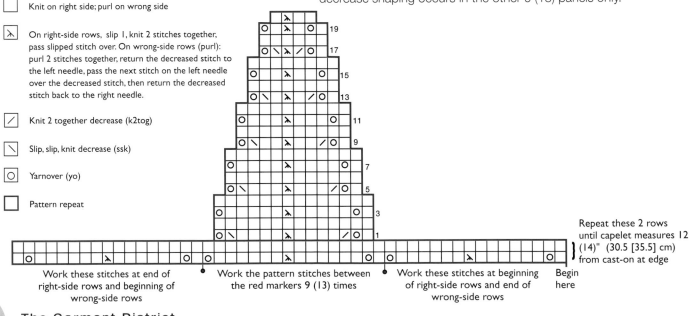

☐ Knit on right side; purl on wrong side

⋏ On right-side rows, slip 1, knit 2 stitches together, pass slipped stitch over. On wrong-side rows (purl): purl 2 stitches together, return the decreased stitch to the left needle, pass the next stitch on the left needle over the decreased stitch, then return the decreased stitch back to the right needle.

╱ Knit 2 together decrease (k2tog)

╲ Slip, slip, knit decrease (ssk)

⊙ Yarnover (yo)

☐ Pattern repeat

Work these stitches at end of right-side rows and beginning of wrong-side rows

Work the pattern stitches between the red markers 9 (13) times

Work these stitches at beginning of right-side rows and end of wrong-side rows

Begin here

Repeat these 2 rows until capelet measures 12 (14)" (30.5 [35.5] cm) from cast-on at edge

Shape shoulders

Row 1: *(right side)* Knit 1, yo, knit 6, sl 1, k2tog, psso, knit 6, yo, (knit 1, yo, k2tog, knit 4, sl 1, k2tog, psso, knit 4, ssk, yo) 9 (13) times, knit 1, yo, knit 6, sl 1, k2tog, psso, knit 6, yo, knit 1—159 (215) stitches remain.

Row 2 and all wrong-side rows through Row 18: Purl.

Row 3: Knit 1, yo, knit 6, sl 1, k2tog, psso, knit 6, yo, (knit 1, yo, knit 5, sl 1, k2tog, psso, knit 5, yo) 9 (13) times, knit 1, yo, knit 6, sl 1, k2tog, psso, knit 6, yo, knit 1.

Row 5: Knit 1, yo, knit 6, sl 1, k2tog, psso, knit 6, yo, (knit 1, yo, k2tog, knit 3, sl 1, k2tog, psso, knit 3, ssk, yo) 9 (13) times, knit 1, yo, knit 6, sl 1, k2tog, psso, knit 6, yo, knit 1—141 (189) stitches remain.

Row 7: Knit 1, yo, knit 6, sl 1, k2tog, psso, knit 6, yo, (knit 1, yo, knit 4, sl 1, k2tog, psso, knit 4, yo) 9 (13) times, knit 1, yo, knit 6, sl 1, k2tog, psso, knit 6, yo, knit 1.

Row 9: Knit 1, yo, knit 6, sl 1, k2tog, psso, knit 6, yo, (k1, yo, k2tog, k2, sl 1, k2tog, psso, k2, ssk, yo) 9 (13) times, k1, yo, knit 6, sl 1, k2tog, psso, knit 6, yo, k1—123 (163) stitches remain.

Row 11: Knit 1, yo, knit 6, sl 1, k2tog, psso, knit 6, yo, (knit 1, yo, knit 3, sl 1, k2tog, psso, knit 3, yo) 9 (13) times, knit 1, yo, knit 6, sl 1, k2tog, psso, knit 6, yo, knit 1.

Row 13: Knit 1, yo, knit 6, sl 1, k2tog, psso, knit 6, yo, (knit 1, yo, k2tog, knit 1, sl 1, k2tog, psso, knit 1, ssk, yo) 9 (13) times, knit 1, yo, knit 6, sl 1, k2tog, psso, knit 6, yo, knit 1—105 (137) stitches remain.

Row 15: Knit 1, yo, knit 6, sl 1, k2tog, psso, knit 6, yo, (knit 1, yo, knit 2, sl 1, k2tog, psso, knit 2, yo) 9 (13) times, knit 1, yo, knit 6, sl 1, k2tog, psso, knit 6, yo, knit 1.

Row 17: Knit 1, yo, knit 6, sl 1, k2tog, psso, knit 6, yo, (knit 1, yo, k2tog, sl 1, k2tog, psso, ssk, yo) 9 (13) times, knit 1, yo, knit 6, sl 1, k2tog, psso, knit 6, yo, knit 1—87 (111) stitches remain.

Row 19: Knit 1, yo, knit 6, sl 1, k2tog, psso, knit 6, yo, (knit 1, yo, knit 1, sl 1, k2tog, psso, knit 1, yo) 9 (13) times, knit 1, yo, knit 6, sl 1, k2tog, psso, knit 6, yo, knit 1.

Row 20: Purl 16, (purl 2, purl 2 together, slip the decreased stitch back to left needle, slip next stitch on left needle over the decreased stitch and drop it from needle, slip the decrease stitch back to right needle, purl 1) 9 (13) times, purl 17 stitches—69 (85) stitches remain.

I-Cord Ties

Don't bind off. Cut yarn leaving a 6" (15-cm) tail, leave stitches on needle and set capelet aside. Using 2 double-pointed needles, cast on 3 stitches for I-cord. Work I-cord for 15" (38 cm). With right side of capelet facing, slip the 3 I-cord stitches onto the capelet needle; the I-cord working yarn will be between the I-cord and capelet stitches. Pull the working yarn across the back of the I-cord stitches to the front of the left needle (needle holding capelet stitches). *With one double-pointed needle in right hand, knit 2 I-cord stitches, work the ssk decrease (you'll be using the third I-cord stitch and the first of the capelet stitches); return the 3 I-cord stitches to the capelet needle (ahead of the capelet stitches) and repeat from * until all the capelet stitches are worked into the attached I-cord bind-off. Don't bind off remaining I-cord stitches. Using both double-pointed needles again, continue working I-cord same as other tie; when tie measures 15" (38 cm) from end of capelet, work last row as sl 1, k2tog, psso. Cut yarn leaving a 4" (10-cm) tail and thread through remaining stitch, pull end to fasten off.

Finishing

Weave in the loose yarn ends with a tapestry needle. Lay capelet flat on a blocking surface, slightly stretching the capelet to smooth the stitch pattern and open up the yarnovers. Lightly spray capelet with water and pin into shape. Smooth out lower edge points and pin in place. Allow to air-dry before moving.

The Skirt

An unexpected knitted garment, this lovely skirt will become a staple in your wardrobe. You might, however, want to wear a slip under it.

Design

Grace Anna Robbins

Finished Size

About 27 (29, 31, 33, 35, 37, 39)" (68.5 [73.5, 78.5, 84, 89, 94, 99] cm) circumference at waist, 30½ (32½, 35, 37½, 39½, 41½, 44)" (77.5 [83, 89, 94.5, 100.5, 105.5, 112] cm) circumference at hip (measured 6" [15 cm] down from bind-off row), and 24" (61 cm) long. Skirt shown measures 33" (84 cm) at waist.

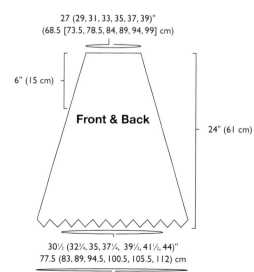

27 (29, 31, 33, 35, 37, 39)"
(68.5 [73.5, 78.5, 84, 89, 94, 99] cm)

6" (15 cm)

Front & Back

24" (61 cm)

30½ (32¾, 35, 37¼, 39½, 41½, 44)"
77.5 (83, 89, 94.5, 100.5, 105.5, 112) cm

81 (87, 93, 99, 105, 111, 117)"
206 (221, 249, 251.5, 267, 282, 287) cm

Materials

Yarn: CYCA classification: 4 Medium; about 980 (1078, 1176, 1176, 1274, 1274, 1372) yards (900 [990, 1080, 1080, 1170, 1170, 1260] meters).

Shown here: Rowan All-Seasons Cotton (60% cotton, 40% acrylic; 98 yards [90 meters]/ 50 grams): #204 remote, 10 (11, 12, 12, 13, 13, 14) skeins; #211 blackcurrant, 1 skein, for intarsia diamond pattern on pocket; #219 dusk, 1 skein, for I-cord belt.

Needles: Size 8 (5 mm) 24" (60 cm) and 32" (80 cm) circular needles. Adjust needle size if necessary to obtain the correct gauge.

Notions: Stitch markers; measuring tape; tapestry needle; four ⅝" (1.5-cm) buttons; large yarn bobbin for pocket.

Gauge

16-stitch repeat = 3" (7.5 cm); 4-stitch repeat = 1" (2.5 cm).

Need to know

Cast on (page 18)
Knit stitch (page 20)
Purl stitch (page 22)
Bind off (page 26)
Join a new ball (page 27)
Weave in ends (page 27)
Blocking (page 28)
Place markers (page 49)
Pass slip stitch over (page 50)
Backward loop cast-on (page 52)
Decreases (page 54)
Knitting in the round (page 57)
I-cord (page 89)

Abbreviations

psso: Pass slip stitch over (page 50)

sl 1: Slip 1 stitch knitwise (page 50)

yo: Yarnover (page 53)

k2tog: Knit 2 stitches together (page 54)

ssk: Slip, slip, knit decrease (page 55)

Basic 16-Stitch Pattern:

Round 1: (right side) *Knit 1, yarnover, knit 6, sl 1, k2tog, psso, knit 6, yarnover; repeat from * to end of round.

Round 2: Knit.

Repeat Rounds 1 and 2 for 16-stitch pattern.

Tip: Read through the instructions and highlight all numbers that apply to the size you plan to make. To learn more about following and reading knitting charts, follow each text row and compare with the chart rows.

Skirt

Cast on 432 (464, 496, 528, 560, 592, 624) stitches loosely. Place stitch marker to denote beginning of round and join for working in the round. Work the basic 16-stitch repeat pattern (at left) until piece measures 3" (7.5 cm) from cast-on edge (measure from the point of the panel), ending with a Round 2 (this means you complete the knit round before starting the next instructions).

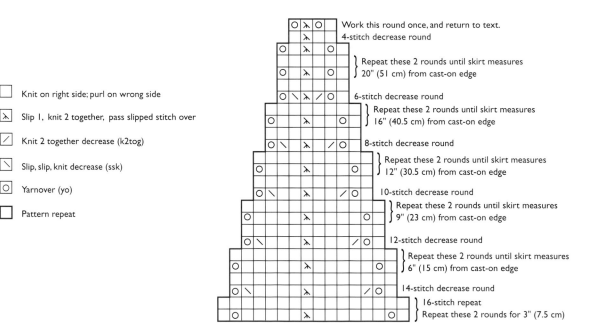

Knit on right side; purl on wrong side

Slip 1, knit 2 together, pass slipped stitch over

Knit 2 together decrease (k2tog)

Slip, slip, knit decrease (ssk)

Yarnover (yo)

Pattern repeat

Decrease to 14-stitch repeat

Round 1: (Knit 1, yo, k2tog, knit 4, sl 1, k2tog, psso, knit 4, ssk, yo) 27 (29, 31, 33, 35, 37, 39) times—378 (406, 434, 462, 490, 518, 546) stitches remain.

Round 2: Knit.

Round 3: (Knit 1, yo, knit 5, sl 1, k2tog, psso, knit 5, yo) 27 (29, 31, 33, 35, 37, 39) times.

Round 4: Knit.

Repeat Rounds 3 and 4 until piece measures 6" (15 cm) from cast-on edge.

Decrease to 12-stitch repeat

Round 1: (Knit 1, yo, k2tog, knit 3, sl 1, k2tog, psso, knit 3, ssk, yo) 27 (29, 31, 33, 35, 37, 39) times—324 (348, 372, 396, 420, 444, 468) stitches remain.

Round 2: Knit.

Round 3: (Knit 1, yo, knit 4, sl 1, k2tog, psso, knit 4, yo) 27 (29, 31, 33, 35, 37, 39) times.

Rounds 4: Knit.

Repeat Rounds 3 and 4 until piece measures 9" (23 cm) from cast-on edge.

Decrease to 10-stitch repeat

Round 1: (Knit 1, yo, k2tog, knit 2, sl 1, k2tog, psso, knit 2, ssk, yo) 27 (29, 31, 33, 35, 37, 39) times—270 (290, 310, 330, 350, 370, 390) stitches remain.

Round 2: Knit.

Round 3: (Knit 1, yo, knit 3, sl 1, k2tog, psso, knit 3, yo) 27 (29, 31, 33, 35, 37, 39) times.

Round 4: Knit.

Repeat Rounds 3 and 4 until piece measures 12" (30.5 cm) from cast-on edge.

Decrease to 8-stitch repeat

Round 1: (Knit 1, yo, k2tog, knit 1, sl 1, k2tog, psso, knit 1, ssk, yo) 27 (29, 31, 33, 35, 37, 39) times—216 (232, 248, 264, 280, 296, 312) stitches remain.

Round 2: Knit.

Round 3: (Knit 1, yo, knit 2, sl 1, k2tog, psso, knit 2, yo) 27 (29, 31, 33, 35, 37, 39) times.

Round 4: Knit.

Repeat Rounds 3 and 4 until piece measures 16" (40.5 cm) from cast-on edge.

Decrease to 6-stitch repeat

Round 1: (Knit 1, yo, k2tog, sl 1, k2tog, psso, ssk, yo) 27 (29, 31, 33, 35, 37, 39) times—162 (174, 186, 198, 210, 222, 234) stitches remain.

Round 2: Knit.

Round 3: (Knit 1, yo, knit 1, sl 1, k2tog, psso, knit 1, yo) 27 (29, 31, 33, 35, 37, 39) times.

Round 4: Knit.

Repeat Rounds 3 and 4 until piece measures 20" (51 cm) from cast-on edge, then work Round 3 once more.

Decrease to 4-stitch repeat

Round 1: (Knit 2, sl 1, k2tog, psso, knit 1) 27 (29, 31, 33, 35, 37, 39) times—108 (116, 124, 132, 140, 148, 156) stitches remain.

Round 2: (Knit 1, yo, sl 1, k2tog, psso, yo) 26 (28, 30, 33, 34, 36, 38) times, then work the last repeat as: (knit 1, yo, sl 1, k2tog, psso, cast on 3 stitches using the backward loop method—the first cast-on stitch will later be worked as the pattern yo)—110 (118, 126, 134, 142, 150, 158) stitches.

Turn row to wrong side and begin working back and forth in rows as follows.

Placket and side opening

Row 1: (wrong side) Purl.

Row 2: (Knit 1, yo, sl 1, k2tog, psso, yo) 27 (29, 31, 33, 35, 37, 39) times, end k2.

Repeat Rows 1 and 2 until placket and side opening measures about 4" (10 cm), ending having completed a right-side row.

Turn work, loosely bind off all stitches purlwise.

Finishing

Weave in loose yarn ends with a tapestry needle. Sew the buttons evenly spaced onto the 2-stitch placket edge to correspond with the open yarnovers on other side of opening. The yarnover eyelets will serve as buttonholes. Block to size.

Make a two-color intarsia pocket (page 116), if desired, and sew to skirt.

I-cord belt

Using yarn color of your choice and two double-pointed needles, cast on 3 stitches and work I-cord for about 72" (183 cm), or desired length. Work last row as sl 1, k2tog, psso—1 stitch remains. Cut yarn leaving 4" (10-cm) tail and use tail to secure last stitch. Thread tail on tapestry needle and insert through center of I-cord. Remove needle. Loosely weave belt in and out yarnover eyelets about two rows down from the bind-off edge.

STUNNINGLY SIMPLE SWEATER STUDIO:
The Pullover and Cardigan

Sweaters, don't you feel cozy just thinking about them? Now, imagine knitting your own in a color you love, a yummy yarn, and in a style that flatters your figure perfectly? It blows your mind, doesn't it? The following two sweaters are based on the same basic pattern and use the same gauge, but with different necklines and sleeves, you can give an entirely unique feel to a garment. Someone else may have created these patterns but remember that you are a design partner in the knitting process. You choose the yarn, the size, and any embellishments. You can also decide to modify the length of the sweater or the sleeves or change the neckline. If you are hesitant about this, seek out an experienced knitter or someone at your local yarn shop and they can help you customize your dream sweater (knitters are nice that way!). Since you're making it, shouldn't it be exactly what you want?

The Go-To Pullover

You'll reach for this sweater again and again. Much like coveted boyfriend sweaters, it's roomy, but this one is made to fit a woman's body. Knitted with a medium-weight wool yarn, this pullover will keep you warm year-round while eliciting envy from your friends. Don't be surprised if a girlfriend (or even your mom!) begs you to make her one in your spare time.

Finished Size

34 (38, 42, 46)" (86.5 [96.5, 106.5, 117] cm) bust circumference. Sweater shown measures 34" (86.5 cm).

Note: The finished sizes are the final measurements across the bust. Therefore, if you measure your bust and it is 34" (86.5 cm), do not make a 34" (86.5 cm) sweater unless you want it skin tight. Make a 38" (96.5 cm) sweater for an average fit, or 42" (106.5) for an oversized fit. Likewise, if you want a tight, 1950s sweater-girl sweater, make your exact size or one size smaller; but beware that it could be too tight in the underarm or too short in the sleeve.

Materials

Yarn: CYCA classification: 4 Medium; about 880 (880, 1100, 1320) yards (804 [804, 1005, 1206] meters.

Shown here: Cascade 220 (100% wool; 220 yards [201 meters]/100 grams). #9407 olive green heather, 4 (4, 5, 6) skeins.

Needles: Size 8 (5 mm): 16" (40 cm) and 24" (60 cm) circular needles and set of 4 or 5 double-pointed. Adjust needle size if necessary to obtain the correct gauge.

Notions: 8 stitch markers; stitch holders; tapestry needle.

Gauge

18 stitches and 24 rows = 4" (10 cm) in stockinette stitch.

Design

Courtney Kelley

Need to know

Cast on (page 18)
Knit stitch (page 20)
Purl stitch (page 22)
Ribbing (page 25)
Bind off (page 26)
Weave in ends (page 27)
Blocking (page 28)
Place markers (page 49)
Place stitches on holder (page 50)
Increases (page 52)
Decreases (page 54)
Knitting in the round (page 57)

Abbreviations

k1f&b: Knit into front and back loop
  of same stitch (page 52)

M1: Make 1 increase (page 53)

k2tog: Knit 2 stitches together (page 54)

ssk: Slip, slip, knit decrease (page 55)

Body

Using longer circular needle, cast on 136 (152, 168, 184) stitches. Place a stitch marker and join for working in the round. Marker denotes side "seam." Slip marker every round.

Work knit 2, purl 2 ribbing until piece measures 2½" (6.5 cm) from cast-on. Change to stockinette stitch (knit every round) and increase 16 (16, 20, 20) stitches evenly spaced (in other words, work the increases at even intervals) on the first round, using the k1f&b method—152 (168, 188, 204) stitches total.

Continue even in stockinette stitch until piece measures 14 (15, 15½, 16)" (35.5 [38, 39, 40.5] cm) from cast-on.

Divide for armholes

Knit 62 (70, 80, 86) stitches for the front, knit the next 14 (14, 14, 16) stitches, then place these stitches on a holder for underarms (stitches will later be joined to the sleeve underarm stitches), knit the next 62 (70, 80, 86) stitches for back, then knit the next 14 (14, 14, 16) stitches and place on a holder for underarm to be joined later to second sleeve. Set body aside.

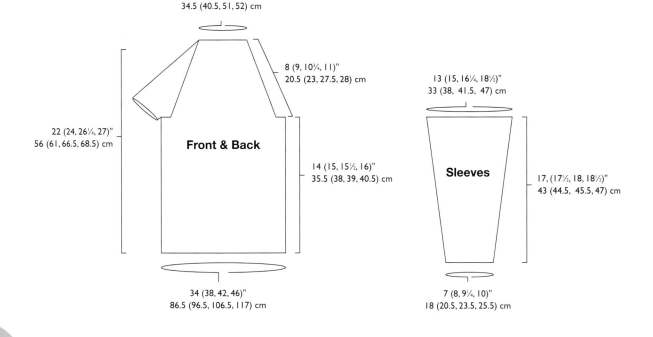

13½ (16, 20, 20½)"
34.5 (40.5, 51, 52) cm

8 (9, 10¾, 11)"
20.5 (23, 27.5, 28) cm

13 (15, 16¼, 18½)"
33 (38, 41.5, 47) cm

22 (24, 26¼, 27)"
56 (61, 66.5, 68.5) cm

Front & Back

14 (15, 15½, 16)"
35.5 (38, 39, 40.5) cm

Sleeves

17, (17½, 18, 18½)"
43 (44.5, 45.5, 47) cm

34 (38, 42, 46)"
86.5 (96.5, 106.5, 117) cm

7 (8, 9¼, 10)"
18 (20.5, 23.5, 25.5) cm

Sleeve (make 2)

Using double-pointed needles, cast on 32 (40, 42, 46) stitches. Arrange stitches as evenly as possible on 3 or 4 needles, join for working in the round, and place a marker to denote end of round. Slip marker every round.

Work knit 2, purl 2 ribbing until piece measures 2½" (6.5 cm) from cast-on. Change to stockinette stitch and work 4 (6, 6, 0) rounds even.

Increase round: Knit 1, M1, knit to 1 stitch before end of round, M1, knit 1—34 (38, 44, 48) stitches.

Work 5 (4, 4, 5) rounds even.

Repeat the last 6 (5, 5, 6) rounds 12 (15, 15, 16) times more—58 (68, 74, 84) stitches.

Work even (do not increase) in stockinette stitch until piece measures 17 (17½, 18, 18½)" (43 [44.5, 45.5, 47] cm) from cast-on.

Next round: Slip the last 7 (7, 7, 8) stitches of the last round onto a holder, knit the first 7 (7, 7, 8) stitches at beginning of round, then slip them onto the same holder ahead of the other stitches on the holder—14 (14, 14, 16) underarm stitches; knit the remaining 44 (54, 60, 68) stitches for sleeve.

Set sleeve aside. Make another sleeve to match.

Join pieces

Using longer circular needle with body stitches attached, knit across 62 (70, 80, 86) stitches for front, place a marker, knit across 44 (54, 60, 68) stitches of one sleeve, place a marker, knit across 62 (70, 80, 86) stitches for back, place a marker, knit across 44 (54, 60, 68) stitches of second sleeve, place a marker of another color or style to denote the end of round—212 (248, 280, 308) stitches total. Slip markers every round.

Yoke

Work even in stockinette stitch until yoke measures 1¼ (1½, 1¾, 1¾)" (3 [3.8, 4.5, 4.5] cm) from joining round.

Decrease round: Slip marker, *k2tog, knit across front to 2 stitches before next marker (first sleeve marker), ssk, slip marker, k2tog, knit to 2 stitches before next marker (first sleeve, second marker), ssk, slip marker, k2tog, knit across back to 2 stitches before next marker (second sleeve, first marker), ssk, slip marker, k2tog, knit to 2 stitches before next marker (second sleeve, second marker and end of round), ssk—204 (240, 272, 300) stitches remain.

Next round: Knit; make no decreases, slip markers as you come to them.

Repeat the last 2 rounds 18 (21, 24, 26) more times—60 (72, 80, 92) stitches remain, yoke measures about 8 (9, 10¾, 11)" (18 [23, 27.5, 28] cm) from joining round. Remove all markers as you work the last knit round, except for the marker at end of round.

Neck

Work knit 2, purl 2 ribbing until neck measures 7" (18 cm). Loosely bind off all stitches.

Finishing

Turn sweater to wrong side. Working one under-arm at a time, slip the 14 (14, 14, 16) stitches from sleeve underarm stitches onto double-pointed needle; slip the 14 (14, 14, 16) sweater underarm stitches onto another double-pointed needle. With wrong sides of work facing out, and right sides together, place both needles parallel with each other, and hold both in left hand. Join yarn leaving a 6" (15 cm) tail, and with an empty double-pointed needle in your right hand, use the three-needle bind-off method to join the stitches together as follows: *Insert needle point into first stitch on each of the parallel needles in the left hand and knit the 2 stitches to-gether—1 stitch on right needle; repeat from * with the next 2 stitches on left needles, 2 stitches on right needle; insert one of the left needle tips into the first stitch on the right needle and lift it over the second stitch on the right nee-dle and drop from needle (this is the same as binding off 1 stitch); repeat from first * until all underarm stitches are joined and bound off. Cut yarn, thread through last stitch on right needle and fasten off. Repeat the entire process with the sec-ond set of underarm stitches. Use the yarn tails to stitch up any open spaces at the beginning and ending of the bind-off. Weave in the loose yarn ends with a tapestry needle. Turn sweater to right side. Block according to yarn manufacturer's instructions.

Belle of the Ball Cardigan

Lately, cardigans have replaced jackets as warm toppers, making this feminine sweater both pretty and practical. Knitted in a dreamy mohair, this sweater is soft enough to wear alone, but you can also slip it on over a camisole or lacy top for a lovely, snuggly date-night look.

Design
Grace Anna Robbins

Need to know
Cast on (page 18)
Knit stitch (page 20)
Purl stitch (page 22)
Bind off (page 26)
Weave in ends (page 27)
Blocking (page 28)
Place markers (page 49)
Place stitches on holder
    (page 50)
Slip stitch (page 50)
Backward loop cast-on
    (page 52)
Increases (page 52)
Decreases (page 54)
Knitting in the round (page 57)

Finished Size

34 (38, 42, 46)" chest circumference. Sweater shown measures 34" (86.5 cm).

Note: The finished sizes are the final measurements across the bust. Therefore, if you measure your bust and it is 34" (86.5 cm), do not make a 34" (86.5 cm) sweater unless you want it skin tight. Make a 38" (96.5 cm) sweater for an average fit, or 42" (106.5) for an oversized fit. Likewise, if you want a tight, 1950s sweater-girl sweater, make your exact size or one size smaller; but beware that it could be too tight in the underarm or too short in the sleeve.

Materials

Yarn: CYCA classification: 4 Medium; about 755 (906, 1057, 1208) yards (690 [828, 966, 1104] meters).

Shown here: GGH Soft Kid, (70% super kid mohair, 25% nylon, 5% wool; 151 yards [138 meters]/25 grams): #72 baby blue, 5 (6, 7, 8) skeins.

Needles: Size 8 (5 mm): 24" (60 cm) and 32" (82 cm) circular needles, and set of 5 double-pointed needles. Adjust needle size if necessary to obtain the correct gauge.

Notions: 5 (6, 7, 8) buttons, about ⅝" (1.5 cm) diameter; stitch markers; stitch holders; tapestry needle; matching sewing thread and sewing needle for buttons if holes are too small to handle yarn.

Gauge

18 stitches and 24 rows = 4" (10 cm) in stockinette stitch.

Abbreviations

M1: Make 1 increase (page 53)

yo: Yarnover (page 53)

k2tog: Knit 2 stitches together decrease (page 54)

ssk: Slip, slip, knit decrease (page 55)

Body

Using 24" (60 cm) circular needle, cast on 136 (152, 168, 184) stitches as follows: cast on 34 (38, 42, 46) stitches, place marker, cast on 68 (76, 84, 92) stitches, place marker, cast on 34 (38, 42, 46) stitches. Do not join into a round, but work back and forth in rows as if you were working on straight needles, slip markers every row.

Note: Slip the first stitch purlwise at the beginning of each row to create a selvedge stitch at the center front edges.

Slipping the first stitch of every row, work garter stitch (knit every row) until piece measures about 1½" (3.8 cm) from cast-on. Beginning with a knit row, change to stockinette stitch (knit right-side rows; purl wrong-side rows) and using the make 1 (M1) method, increase 16 (16, 20, 20) stitches across the first row as follows: increase 4 (4, 5, 5) stitches evenly spaced before the first marker, increase 8 (8, 10, 10) stitches evenly spaced before the next marker, increase 4 (4, 5, 5) stitches evenly spaced before the end of row—152 (168, 188, 204) sts total. Continuing to slip the first stitch in each row, work even in stockinette stitch until piece measures 14½ (15, 15½, 16)" (37 [38, 39, 40.5] cm) from cast-on edge, ending after completing a wrong-side row (purl row).

Divide for armholes

Next row: (right side) Knit 31 (35, 40, 42) stitches, place marker, slip next 14 (14, 14, 18) stitches onto stitch holder (remove original markers when you reach them), knit 62 (70, 80, 84) stitches, place marker, slip next 14 (14, 14, 18) stitches onto another stitch holder, knit 31 (35, 40, 42) stitches to end of row—124 (140, 160, 168) stitches remain. Set body aside.

Sleeve (make 2)

Using double-pointed needles, cast on 44 (46, 48, 50) stitches. Arrange stitches as evenly as possible on four needles, join for working in the round, and place a marker to denote end of round. Slip marker every round.

Work garter stitch (alternate knit 1 round, purl 1 round) until piece measures 1" (2.5 cm) from cast-on. Change to stockinette stitch (knit every round).

Increase round: Knit 1, M1, knit to last stitch, M1, knit 1— 46 (48, 50, 52) stitches.

Knit 7 (5, 4, 3) rounds.

Repeat the last 8 (6, 5, 4) rounds 7 (10, 12, 15) more times, then work even until sleeve measures 12 (12½, 13, 13½)" (30.5 [31.5, 33, 34.5] cm) from cast-on—60 (68, 74, 82) stitches.

Next round: Slip the last 7 (7, 7, 9) stitches of the last round onto a holder, knit the first 7 (7, 7, 9) stitches at the beginning of the round and slip them onto the same holder (14 [14, 14, 18] underarm stitches). Knit the remaining 46 (54, 60, 64) stitches for sleeve. Set sleeve aside. Make another sleeve to match.

Join pieces

Using the circular needle holding the body stitches knit across 31 (35, 40, 42) stitches for right front, place a marker, knit across 46 (54, 60, 64) stitches of one sleeve, place a marker, knit across 62 (70, 80, 84) stitches for back, place a marker, knit across 46 (54, 60, 64) stitches of other sleeve, place a marker, then knit across 31 (35, 40, 42) for left front—216 (248, 280, 296) stitches total. Slip markers every row. (Use longer circular needle if necessary for larger sizes.)

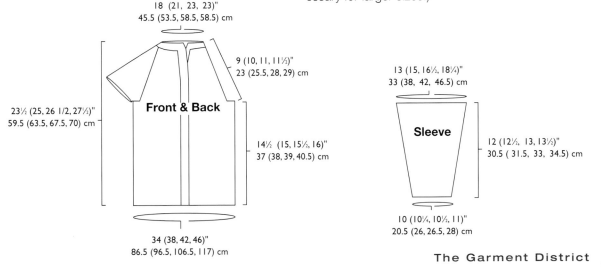

18 (21, 23, 23)"
45.5 (53.5, 58.5, 58.5) cm

9 (10, 11, 11½)"
23 (25.5, 28, 29) cm

23½ (25, 26 1/2, 27½)"
59.5 (63.5, 67.5, 70) cm

Front & Back

14½ (15, 15½, 16)"
37 (38, 39, 40.5) cm

34 (38, 42, 46)"
86.5 (96.5, 106.5, 117) cm

13 (15, 16½, 18¼)"
33 (38, 42, 46.5) cm

Sleeve

12 (12½, 13, 13½)"
30.5 (31.5, 33, 34.5) cm

10 (10¼, 10½, 11)"
20.5 (26, 26.5, 28) cm

Yoke

Beginning with a wrong-side (purl) row, work even in stockinette stitch until yoke measures 1¼ (1½, 1¾, 1¾)" (3 [4, 4.5, 4.5] cm) from joining row, ending with a wrong-side (purl) row.

Decrease row (right side): Knit across right front stitches to 2 stitches before first marker, ssk, slip marker, k2tog, knit across stitches of first sleeve to 2 stitches before next marker, ssk, slip marker, k2tog, knit across stitches of back to 2 stitches before next marker, ssk, slip marker, k2tog, knit across stitches of second sleeve, ssk, slip marker, k2tog, knit to end of row—208 (240, 272, 288) stitches remain.

Next 3 rows: Work in stockinette stitch, beginning with a purl row.

Repeat the last 4 rows 2 (2, 1, 0) more time(s)—192 (224, 264, 288) stitches remain.

Next row (right side): Repeat decrease row—184 (216, 256, 280) stitches remain.

Next row: Purl.

Repeat the last 2 rows 13 (15, 19, 22) more times—80 (96,104,104) stitches remain. Leave stitches and markers on needle. Cut yarn, leaving a 6" (15-cm) tail.

Pick Up and Knit

With right side of work facing and working from right to left, insert needle tip into the edge stitch, wrap the yarn around the needle, and pull it through the edge stitch to create one stitch on the needle.

Front and Neck Band

Note: After picking up and knitting the center front band stitches, smooth out the band stitches to make sure the band lays flat against the center front edge. The numbers provided below are based on the row gauge, but if the project was lengthened or shortened, or the first stitches of each row weren't slipped, or the work isn't exactly to gauge, then you'll need to make an adjustment in the number of stitches picked up. If the band puckers or pulls, add some extra stitches; if it's wavy, that indicates there are too many stitches, so delete a few. If adjustments are needed, make them now, or on the next wrong-side row. It's important that the front bands and the cardigan fronts are the same length, and that the bands lie flat.

The front and neck band is worked as one piece in garter stitch (knit every row); the increases at the mitered corners are made using the backward loop method. With the longer circular needle and right side of work facing, join yarn to right front at the center front cast-on edge. Pick up and knit (see box below left) 1 stitch in each of the center front slipped stitches—about 66 (72, 76, 78) stitches.

Join to neck stitches

Using the backward loop method, increase 1 stitch, place marker, knit 1 stitch from the body stitches, place marker, increase 1, knit across front to 2 stitches before next marker, ssk, slip marker, knit across sleeve to 2 stitches before next marker, ssk, slip marker, knit across back to 2 stitches before next marker, ssk, slip marker, knit across second sleeve to 2 stitches before marker, ssk, slip marker, knit to 1 stitch before end of row, increase 1 stitch using the backward loop method, place marker, knit 1, place marker, increase 1 as before, pick up and knit 66 (72, 76, 78) stitches working into the slipped stitches along the left front to the cast-on edge—212 (248, 256, 260) stitches. (If you made a stitch count adjustment along the right front band, make sure you pick up the same number of stitches on the left front.)

Row 2: (wrong side) Knit all stitches, slipping markers as you reach them.

Row 3: (right side) Knit to first marker at neck edge, increase 1, slip marker, knit 1, slip marker, increase 1, knit to 2 stitches before next marker, ssk, slip marker, knit to 2 stitches before next marker, ssk, slip marker, knit to 2 stitches before next marker, ssk, slip marker, knit to 2 stitches before next marker, ssk, slip marker, knit to next marker, increase 1, slip marker, knit 1, slip marker, increase 1, knit to end of row.

Repeat Rows 2 and 3 once more, then work Row 2 once more.

Buttonhole row: (right side) Place the first buttonhole about 1" (2.5 cm) up from the cast-on edge, k2tog, yo (first buttonhole made), *place the next buttonhole about 1¾ (2, 2½, 2½)" (4.5 [5, 6.5, 6.5] cm) from the previous one, k2tog, yo; repeat from * 4 (5, 6, 7) more times; knit to next marker, increase 1 (backward loop method), slip marker, knit 1, slip marker, increase 1, knit to 2 stitches before next marker, ssk, slip marker, knit to 2 stitches before next marker, ssk, slip marker, knit to 2 stitches before next marker, ssk, slip marker, knit to 2 stitches before next marker, ssk, slip marker, knit to next marker, increase 1, slip marker, knit 1, slip marker, increase 1, knit to end of row.

Repeat Rows 2 and 3 two more times (4 rows total). Loosely bind off all stitches.

Finishing

Weave in loose ends with a tapestry needle. Turn cardigan to wrong side. Working one underarm at a time, slip the 14 (14, 14, 18) stitches from sleeve underarm stitches onto double-pointed needle; slip the 14 (14, 14, 18) cardigan underarm stitches onto another double-pointed needle. With wrong sides of work facing out, and right sides together, place both needles parallel with each other, and hold both in left hand. Join yarn leaving a 6" (15-cm) tail, and with an empty double-pointed needle in your right hand, work the three-needle method to bind off the stitches together as follows: *Insert needle point into first stitch on each of the parallel needles in the left hand and knit the 2 stitches together, 1 stitch on right needle; repeat from * with the next 2 stitches on left needles, 2 stitches on right needle; insert one of the left needle tips into the first stitch on the right needle and lift it over the second stitch on the right needle and drop from needle (this is the same as binding off 1 stitch); repeat from first * until all underarm stitches are joined and bound off. Cut yarn, thread through last stitch on right needle and fasten off. Repeat the entire process with the second set of underarm stitches. Use the yarn tails to stitch up any open spaces at the beginning and ending of the bind-off. Weave the remaining loose ends through stitches on the wrong side of work. Turn cardigan to right side. Align both center front bands with right front (as worn) over left front. With pins, mark spacing for buttons on left front (as worn) to match button holes on right front. With yarn threaded on tapestry needle, or sewing thread and sewing needle, attach buttons to left front band. Block according to yarn manufacturer's instructions.

The Big Finish

You've graduated from quizzes! The only question left to answer is, "What do I knit next?" At this point, you may still be getting comfortable reading patterns, let alone manipulating two pointed sticks.

You are well into a journey that can offer you a lifetime of excitement, challenges, and yep, frustration. But with every roadblock, there's a new avenue to show you something new. And to that point, this chapter presents a variety of embellishments that you can use to personalize your knitting. Learn to create fringe and edge a tunic with it. Tie a couple of small pompoms to the ends of I-cord you've created to keep your mittens together. With these

flourishes, you can take any pattern and create something utterly new and unique.

To help expand your horizon, we'll show you how to embellish some of the projects in this book. Don't stop with our ideas, however. Go crazy and add a pocket to a baby blanket or leaves all over a cap or show some restraint and knit a classic scarf you'll have and wear to death. Again, it's all up to you!

Ladder Scarf (page 36)

Fringe is a great way to add pizzazz to scarves, but you can also put fringe on blankets, shawls, and sweaters. And it's easy-peasy to boot!

Step 1: Cut a piece of cardboard about an inch longer than the desired length of your fringe. Starting from the bottom edge, wrap yarn around the cardboard once for each strand of fringe you want to create. Make sure you account for all the edges you want to fringe (two ends of a scarf, for example).

Step 2: When you have the desired amount of fringe wrapped around the cardboard, end your wrapping on the bottom edge (the same edge that you started with). With sharp scissors, cut along the bottom edge between the cardboard and the yarn (Figure 1). Do not cut along the top edge.

Step 3: Slip a crochet hook through the first row above the edge of your knitting from front to back. Fold the strands in half and place them on the hook. Pull the hook up and through the main piece so that a loop of the fringe yarn appears (Figure 2).

Step 4: Remove the hook and slip the loose ends of the strands through the loop, adjust the strand placement so that the loose ends hang off the edge of the piece, and pull tight.

It's a snap, right? Now just repeat this along the edge of your work until you feel your garment is fringed to your satisfaction, and enjoy.

If you really want to get crazy, you can knot strands together to create a fancy fringe that would be right at home in the heart of Haight Ashbury (Figure 3).

FRINGE

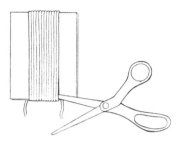

Figure 1. Cut the bottom edge of the yarn wrapped around cardboard.

Figure 2. Pull a loop of fringe yarn through the edge of the knitted piece.

Figure 3. Slip the loose strands through the loop, then knot the fringe ends together for a bohemian effect.

Cable Cap (page 76)

POM-POMS

Pom-poms are not just for cheerleaders! Haven't you always wanted pom-poms of your own? You don't need a big set of pom-poms to shake for the team—you can top a hat and shake that in someone's direction instead.

Step 1: Cut a piece of sturdy cardboard that is the same width (or diameter) as the desired size of your pom-pom. Wrap yarn around the cardboard until it's really full.

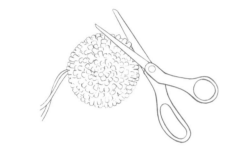

Step 2: Carefully slip the cardboard out from the yarn. Cut a 12" (30.5-cm) piece of yarn, and tie it around the middle of your wrapped yarn. Make it tight and knot it securely. Leave a long tail to secure your pom-pom to your work.

Step 3: Cut both ends of the wrapped yarn, fluff like crazy, trim the ends to the same length, and tie your pom-pom to whatever you please.

BLANKET STITCH

Adding a cool edging to any knitted work can give it an extra polish that will make it look completely unique and, at the same time, totally professional. **Blanket stitch** is a homespun edging that lends a kind of frontier spirit to your garment. Giddyup!

Cut a length of yarn about five times longer than the area you are edging.

Super Hero Hand Huggers (page 44)

Step 1: Working along the edge closest to you, insert the needle from back to front about 2 rows from the edge (or about ¼" [6 mm]), leaving a 4" (10-cm) tail on the wrong side to weave in later.

Step 2: Holding the working yarn along the lower edge, move to the right about ¼" (6 mm) and 2 rows from the edge, insert the needle into the stitch from front to back, bring the needle down toward the lower edge passing over the yarn at the lower edge, and pull gently to close.

Repeat Step 2 for the desired number of stitches. On the last stitch, pull the yarn through the lower edge of the first blanket stitch and connect the first and last stitches together. Turn work to wrong side and weave in the loose yarn ends through several stitches.

If you're working blanket stitch over ribbing, insert the needle into the knit stitches and work as above, skipping the purl stitches.

Yeah, yeah, you just learned to knit and now we want you to *crochet*? No, we're not kidding. **Crocheting** an edge on your work is a snap (you'll enter a zen state as you get into a groove) and a crocheted edge adds a crisp, feminine, or elegant finish to your project.

Step 1: With right side of work facing and keeping the working yarn on the wrong side of the work, insert the hook into the knitted fabric, grab a loop of yarn with the crochet hook and draw it through to the right side.

Step 2: Insert the hook into the next stitch from front to back, yarn over, and draw a loop through the knit fabric and the loop on the crochet hook.

Step 3: Move forward one or more stitches, then repeat Step 2.

Repeat Steps 2 and 3 for the desired distance. Cut yarn leaving 4" (10-cm) tail, thread through to right side and pull through last loop on hook to secure. Take yarn to wrong side and weave in end through several stitches to secure.

CROCHET CHAIN STITCH BORDER

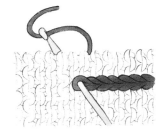

Crochet a chain stitch border by pulling loops of yarn through each other.

Stop Sign Baby Blanket (page 63)

CARING FOR YOUR CREATIONS

Now that you've knit a thing or two, you probably want to make sure you take care of it. While this includes making sure you don't slam the door on the end of your tasseled scarf, it also extends to washing and storing your creations. Save the yarn labels (noting what project you used the yarn for); they give general guidelines for washing your knitted item. Many yarns are now machine-washable so take advantage of this great feature when you can, paying close attention to whether you can wash it in hot water or put it in the dryer, both of which can cause shrinkage. If you are unsure of how to care for something, handwashing is the way to go. Use a drop of Eucalan (see page 133) or another wool wash and then lay it flat to air-dry.

When it comes to storing your garments, seal them in an airtight and waterproof container with mothballs or sachets. Avoiding direct sunlight will help prevent fading.

Making Lemonade Out of Lemons

Sometimes a project doesn't turn out the way you envisioned. In fact, it happens all the time. The scarf you thought would be short and wide is long and skinny after blocking. Or the peddler's shawl that took you so long to make has a jog in the pattern smack dab in the center.

But don't despair. While a knitted work may not be what you had in mind, you can choose to go with the flow and create something just as lovely and altogether new.

Mistakes can be camouflaged by embellishment. Knit a flower (see page 120) and sew it over the mistake. Or you don't even have to knit anything extra. Sew a button or pin a funky broach over the error. Make a statement with a campaign pin. Whipstitch the edge of a piece with a contrasting yarn if your bind-off is uneven.

But you don't have to hide the flaw. Embrace it! Treat it as a quirk that gives your piece character and distinction. Chances are, you'll be the only one to detect the problem anyway . . . unless you are prone to pointing it out whenever someone compliments you on your amazing handiwork. Try this instead whenever you feel the urge to downplay your talent: Just say "thank you."

You can embellish your knitting with:

- buttons

- safety pins

- vintage brooches

- statement pins

- stick pins and tie tacks

- pieces of fabric

- beads and charms

- other knitted shapes

- yarn stitched on edges or even woven through a piece

Intarsia Pocket

Design

Grace Anna Robbins

Need to know

Cast on (page 18)

Knit stitch (page 20)

Purl stitch (page 22)

Bind off (page 26)

Weave in ends (page 27)

Knit two together (page 54)

Slip, slip, knit (page 55)

Intarsia (page 59)

Lace Skirt (page 95)

This pocket is a great introduction to intarsia color work. While it is perfectly suited to the Capelet and Skirt patterns (pages 91 and 95, respectively), you can knit this up and adorn bags, shawls, or even a scarf with it.

Finished Size

About 4" (10 cm) wide by 5" (12.5 cm) long at point.

Materials

Yarn: CYCA classification: 4 Medium; small amounts of two colors.

Shown here: Rowan All-Seasons Cotton (60% cotton, 40% acrylic; 98 yards [90 meters]/ 50 grams): #204 remote (main color), #211 blackcurrant (contrasting color), 1 skein each.

Needles: Size 7 (4.5 mm) straight needles. Adjust needle size if necessary to obtain the correct gauge.

Notions: Tapestry needle.

Gauge

9 stitches = 2" (5 cm) in stockinette stitch.

☐ Knit on right side of work; purl on wrong side

· Purl on right side of work; knit on wrong side

◤ Knit 2 together decrease on right side of work

◣ Slip, slip, knit decrease on right side of work

◥ Slip 1, knit 2 together, pass slipped stitch over

■ Knit on right side; purl on wrong side

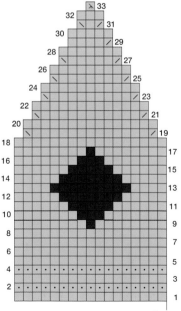

Begin

Pocket

Cut several yards (meters) of main color yarn and wind into a neat little ball to use later.

Using main color yarn from the main ball, cast on 17 stitches.

Knit 4 rows. Beginning with a knit row, work 4 rows in stockinette stitch.

Join contrasting color and work diamond as follows:

Row 9: (right side) Knit 8 with main color, knit 1 with contrasting color, join little ball of yarn and knit 8.

Row 10: (wrong side) Purl 7 with main color (from little ball), purl 3 with contrasting color, purl 7 with main color (from main ball).

Row 11: Knit 6 with main color, knit 5 with contrasting color, knit with 6 main color (from little ball).

Row 12: Purl 5 with main color, purl 7 with contrasting color, purl 5 with main color.

Row 13: Knit 4 with main color, knit 9 with contrasting color, knit 4 with main color.

Row 14: Purl 5 with main color, purl 7 with contrasting color, purl 5 with main color.

Row 15: Knit 6 with main color, knit 5 with contrasting color, knit 6 with main color.

Row 16: Purl 7 with main color, purl 3 with contrasting color, purl 7 with main color.

Row 17: Knit 8 with main color, knit 1 with contrasting color, knit 8 with main color. Cut off little ball of main yarn and contrasting color, leaving 4" (10-cm) tails to weave in later.

Continue with main ball, purl 1 row.

Next row: Knit 2 together, knit to the last 2 stitches, slip, slip, knit decrease—2 stitches decreased.

Next row: Purl.

Repeat the last 2 rows until 3 stitches remain.

Next row: (right side) Slip 1, knit 2 together, pass slipped stitch over—1 stitch remains.

Cut yarn, leaving a 4" (10 cm) tail. Thread tail through last stitch to secure.

Finishing

Weave in ends with a tapestry needle.

Attach pocket to garment

Decide where you'd like your pocket on the skirt, front or back, left side, right side. It's your choice. Keep in mind the skirt side opening should be worn on the left side. So establish where this is by trying on the skirt, and then decide where to place the pocket. Center the point at the bottom of the pocket along the point of one pattern repeat and pin in place with straight pins. Using a tapestry needle threaded with the main color yarn, sew the sides and the bottom edges. Weave in loose ends with a tapestry needle.

Crazy Corkscrew Worm

Design
Lisa R. Myers

Need to know
Cast on (page 18)
Knit stitch (page 20)
Bind off (page 26)
Weave in ends (page 27)
Knit in front and back (page 52)

Use this cute corkscrew as a whimsical embellishment for hats, scarves, sweaters, or any other garment that needs a little something.

Finished Size

About 6 (9)" (15 [23] cm) long.

Materials

Yarn: CYCA classification: 4 Medium; about 15 yards (13.5 meters) for a 9" (23 cm) worm.

Shown here: Plymouth Encore, worsted weight (75% acrylic, 25% wool; 200 yards [180 meters]/100 grams): #9401 light sage.

Needles: Size 8 (5 mm) straight needles. Adjust needle size if necessary to obtain the correct gauge.

Notions: Tapestry needle.

Gauge

4½ stitches = 1" in garter stitch. *Note:* Because of the rapid increase rate, the gauge will not be the same as the Starter Garter Stitch Scarf on page 32, even with the same yarn and needle size. However, gauge isn't important when making the corkscrews.

Starter Garter Scarf (page 32)

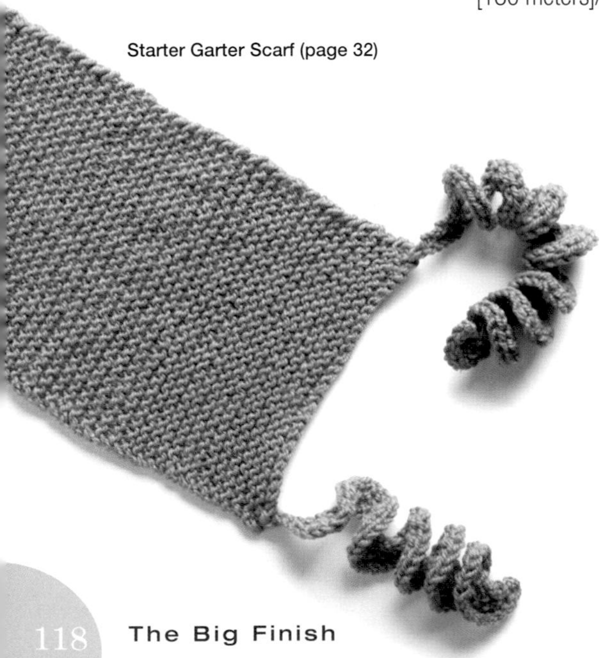

Corkscrew Worm

Cast on 24 (36) stitches.

Row 1: Knit.

Row 2: Knit into the front and back of every stitch—48 (72) stitches.

Row 3: Knit.

Row 4: Knit into the front and back of every stitch—96 (144) stitches.

Row 5: Knit.

Row 6: Bind off all stitches loosely.

Cut yarn, leaving a yarn tail long enough to attach the corkscrew to the project.

Finishing

Weave in loose ends with a tapestry needle.

The Power Flower

Design

Lisa R. Myers

Need to know

Cast on (page 18)

Knit stitch (page 20)

Purl stitch (page 22)

Bind off (page 26)

Weave in ends (page 27)

Knit two together (page 54)

This adorable flower is the perfect finish for a hat, or even a scarf, sweater, or wrap. Experiment with different needle sizes and yarns and you might find all sorts of uses for it.

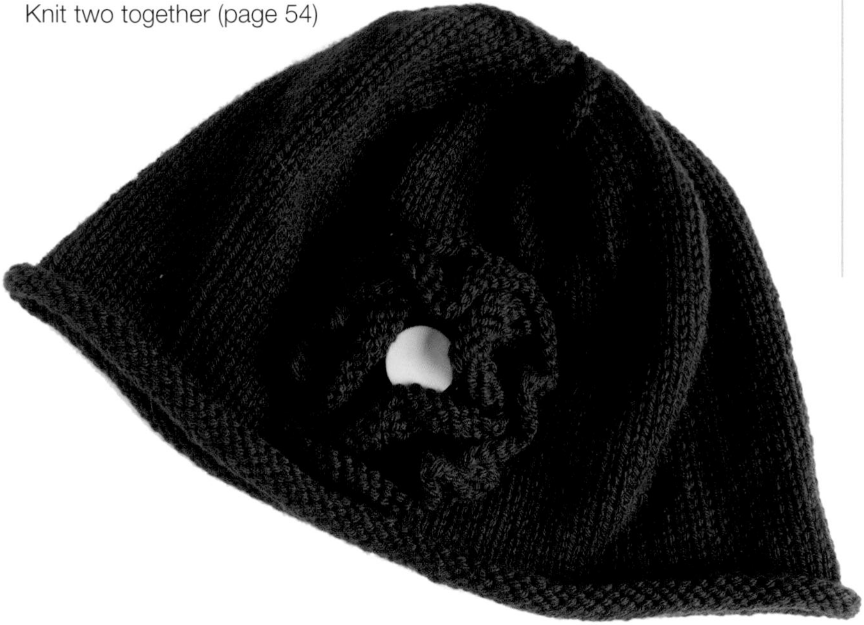

Finished Size

About 3½" (9 cm) in diameter.

Materials

Yarn: CYCA classification: 3 Light; about 20 yards (18 meters).

Shown here: Rowan Cashsoft DK (57% extra fine merino wool, 33% microfiber, 10% cashmere; 143 yards [130 meters]/50 grams): #4513 poison.

Needles: Size 6 (4 mm) straight needles. Adjust needle size if necessary to obtain the correct gauge.

Notions: 1" (2.5-cm) diameter button for center of flower; tapestry needle.

Gauge

5¼ stitches = 1" (2.5 cm) in stockinette stitch.

Rock and Roll Brim Hat (page 74)

Flower

Cast on 160 stitches.

Row 1: Knit.

Row 2: Purl.

Row 3: (Knit 2 together) across row—80 stitches.

Row 4: Purl.

Row 5: (Knit 2 together) across row—40 stitches.

Row 6: Bind off all stitches purlwise.

Finishing

Weave in ends with a tapestry needle. Curl the piece around itself to form 2 or 3 layers of "petals," as shown. With yarn threaded on tapestry needle, tack them in place in several places to maintain the shape. Sew a button in the center.

Accidents Will Happen

Even the most experienced knitter is bound to make a mistake every now and then. The important thing to remember is that most things can be fixed. And if you don't notice a wrong stitch until you've knitted 12" (30.5 cm) of complicated knitting, think of it as an adorable quirk in your work, unless it throws the whole stitch pattern off, or you're a perfectionist, in which case, by all means, rip out your rows and reknit the stitch properly.

I once heard that many artists from the Arts & Crafts movement embraced flaws or asymmetries in their work because it highlighted the unique and the individual craftsman. Think about that when you don't feel quite up to redoing significant chunks of your knitting. View the "mistake" as a charming quirk rather than a niggling mistake.

THE BIGGEST OFFENDER:
Picking Up a Dropped Stitch

It happens to the most careful knitter. You will at some point drop a stitch when you are knitting, meaning a stitch will drop off your needle without your knowing it and the number of stitches on your needle will be reduced by one.

To get a stitch back where it belongs, you must first locate where you dropped the stitch. Knit your row up to the point where you dropped the stitch (Figure 1). With a crochet hook, pick up the loose stitch and weave it up. To do this, place the crochet hook through the stitch and pull it through the strand of yarn above it (Figure 2). Now take the strand above that and pull it through the stitch with the crochet hook. Continue this upwards until you can place the stitch onto the left needle (Figure 3). Work the stitch and the rest of the stitches to the end of the row. Blocking will even out this area if it's tight.

Figure 1. Knit to the dropped stitch.

Figure 2. Use a crochet hook to loop the nearest strand of yarn through the loose stitch.

Figure 3. Continue looping strands one at a time until you can put the final loop on the needle.

When you start to knit a row, it's very easy to knit into the wrong spot and wind up knitting the two bars of a stitch, rather than the stitch itself. How, you might ask? Well, if a stitch is pulled up slightly, it will look like two separate stitches (Figures 1 and 2).

So when starting a row, pull down the knitted fabric so it's all hanging below the needle and pull the working yarn toward you and in front of the needle (Figures 3 and 4). This will help you see the stitches clearly. If you do knit into the wrong spot, you will have to undo the stitches to the beginning of the row and reknit them. If you leave the extra stitches be, your knitting will suddenly get wider on one side, which is probably not the effect you intended.

This will add an extra stitch to your row so as soon as you catch it, undo your stitches until you backtrack to the yarnover, which will leave a gap in your knitting.

You can always decrease a stitch with one of several methods to get back to the right number of stitches, but your stitch pattern will be out of whack. Undo your stitches, pull out the yarnover and pull the yarn into its proper place, and reknit the row.

A LOOP OF A STITCH GETS WRAPPED AND YOU KNIT INTO WRONG SPOT

Figure 1. Misaligned edge stitch can look like two separate stitches.

Figure 2. Align the edge stitch by pulling down on the fabric so it's all below the needle.

Figure 3. Misaligned purl stitch.   Figure 4. Correct purl stitch.

THE ACCIDENTAL YARNOVER

An accidental yarnover will create an extra stitch on the right needle.

PICKING UP YOUR WORK MID-ROW

The working yarn should be attached to the stitches on the right needle.

There will come a time when something or someone interrupts your knitting. You might be forced to put your work down mid-row. If this happens, make sure you slide the stitches far down on the needle so you don't accidentally drop a stitch. When you pick up your work, you might be confused about which needle goes in which hand. Here's a tip: the working yarn will be on the right portion of your fabric.

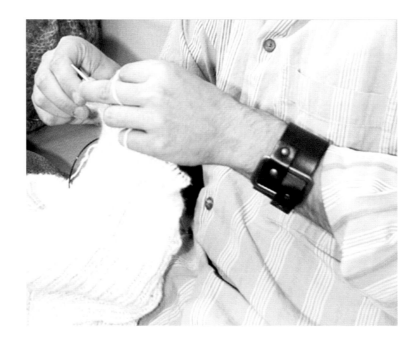

If you are working with a floppy or fuzzy yarn, or only have a few stitches or rows to undo, you may want to do it one stitch at a time. However, if you are working with a firm yarn and have to rip out quite a lot of fabric, you can slip the needle out of your row. Then just gently pull and wrap the yarn back onto your ball (it can get tangled quickly) to the beginning of the mistake row. In other words, rip out the wrong stitch and the rest of the row as well, slip the needle carefully through the stitch loops that will be sticking up, count that you picked them all up, and start reknitting the row (make sure you slip the project needle in so that the pointed end has the working yarn at the end of it). If you're concerned about ripping out too far, you can insert a needle into the work just below the area that needs fixing (Figure 1). To do this, select a smaller size needle than the project size in use, and use a circular or double-pointed one. Insert the needle under the first loop of each stitch and over the second loop across the row, then pull on the working yarn to unravel all the stitches and rows above the needle (Figure 2). When you begin the work again, use your regular size needles to work the stitches.

Which row are you on, you may ask? Well, you have to look at the previous row. And since you are looking at the opposite side of what you just knit, turn your piece around and look at the stitches on the previous row, starting at the right and moving left. Write down if you knit, purled, increased, decreased, or cabled. Now, check out your stitch pattern and see what row matches your findings.

When you put stitches back on a needle, you might slip them on the wrong way. While this doesn't spell disaster for your project, it will slightly twist the stitch. When you knit into the stitch and it feels stiff or tight, you probably put it on the needle incorrectly. The leading leg of the stitch (knit or purl) should be in front of the needle. If the leading leg is at the back of the needle, simply slip the stitch to the right needle and with your left needle, work into the stitch and correct the order of the loop. Slip it back on your left needle and proceed to work it according to the pattern.

RIPPING OUT ROWS

Figure 1. Place a knitting needle into a row of stitches below the area that needs to be ripped out.

Figure 2. You will not be able to rip out stitches once you reach the needle.

The Knitter's Pantry

There are certain tools that should be in every knitter's pantry. Here are the essentials:

yarn

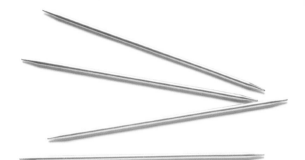

double-pointed needles

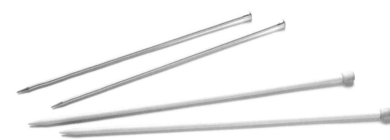

straight needles

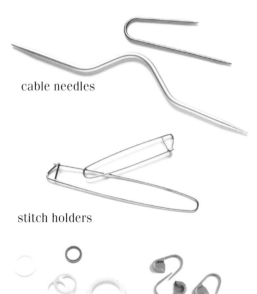

cable needles

stitch holders

ring markers and safety-pin markers

circular needle

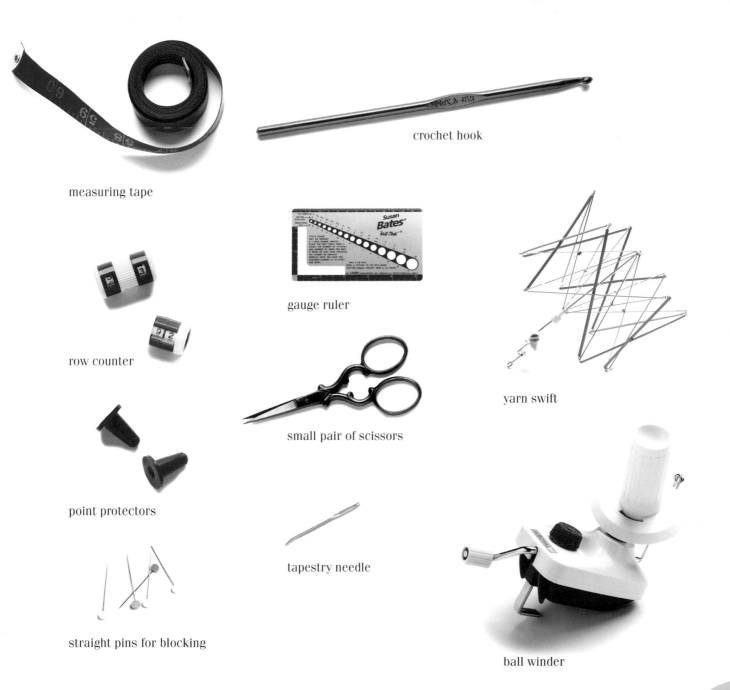

measuring tape

crochet hook

gauge ruler

row counter

yarn swift

small pair of scissors

point protectors

tapestry needle

ball winder

straight pins for blocking

Abbreviations

While there are a lot of abbreviations for knitting cables, lace, or multicolored projects, we used them very sparingly in this book. However, here are some basic abbreviations you'll find in many knitting patterns.

beg	beginning
BO	bind off
CO	cast on
dec	decrease
dpn	double-pointed needle(s)
g	gram(s)
inc	increase, increasing, increases, increased
k	knit
k2tog	knit two stitches together
k1f&b	knit into front and back of stitch
m1	make one (increase)
m1p	make one purl (increase)
mm	millimeters
oz	ounce(s)
p	purl
patt	pattern
pm	place marker
prev	previous
psso	pass slipped stitch over
rem	remaining, remains

rep	repeat, repeated, repeating
rib	ribbing
rnd(s)	round(s)
RS	right side
sl	slip
sl m	slip marker
ssk	slip, slip, knit (a single stitch decrease)
st(s)	stitch(es)
St st	Stockinette stitch
tbl	through back loop(s)
tog	together
WS	wrong side
wyb	with yarn in back (also wyib)
wyf	with yarn in front (also wyif)
yo	yarnover
*	repeat starting point
( )	alternate measurements and/or instructions
[ ]	instructions worked as a group a specified number of times

Glossary

backward loop cast-on: Simple method of casting on stitches. Can be used to create a whole row or adding stitches anywhere within a row. It is also used to make simple increases.

binding off: The technique used to fasten off stitches at the end of a piece of knitting.

blanket stitch: A decorative stitch used in embroidery, typically worked along edges.

blocking: Wetting or steaming a piece of knitting in order to shape it and even out the yarn and stitches.

bulky, or chunky: A category of thick yarns.

cable: A group of stitches knitted out of order to create a twisted, or cabled, effect in your knitting.

cable needle: A short needle used to hold several stitches to the front or the back of your knitting so that you can knit your stitches out of order and create a crossover effect every so often to create a cabled pattern.

casting on: The process of making new stitches on a needle to begin a piece of knitting.

circular needle: A knitting needle with points on each end and a flexible center cord; used to knit in the round or to work a large number of stitches.

crochet chain: An embroidered chain-like stitch worked with a crochet hook.

decrease: One of several techniques used to reduce the number of stitches in order to shape a garment or make it narrower.

DK: A category of lightweight yarn.

double-pointed needle: Aptly named, a dpn is a needle with points on each end used to knit small items, like socks and baby hats, in the round.

dye lot: The batch of yarn that was dyed at the same time. Make sure all of your skeins come from the same dye lot if you want to ensure color consistency in your garment.

ease: The difference between a body's actual measurements and a garment's measurements. The greater the difference, the greater the ease.

Fair Isle: Knitting with two colors in the same row to produce a patterned effect.

felting: The process of agitating a knitted work in hot water to produce a dense fabric.

garter stitch: The pattern created by knitting every row or, if knitting in the round, knitting one round and purling the next.

gauge: The number of stitches and rows in a particular measurement, such as "16 stitches and 20 rows = 4 inches (10 cm)." Checking gauge is critical to achieving a proper fit.

gram: A metric unit used to weigh yarn, equal to .035 ounces.

hank: The coil of yarn ready to be wound into a ball.

I-cord: A sturdy tube of knitting made with double-pointed needles.

increase: One of several techniques used to increase the number of stitches in order to shape a garment or make it wider.

intarsia: A technique that uses different-colored yarns to produce pictures or shapes in a work.

knitting in the round: Knitting continuously in a circle without turning the work; projects are often seamless. Also called "circular" knitting.

knit stitch: The fundamental stitch that looks like interlocking "Vs" when knitted across a row.

make 1 (M1): An increase made between 2 stitches.

meter: A unit of length used to measure yarn, equal to 1.094 yards.

needle gauge: A small flat device with different-sized holes and measurements used for checking needle sizes.

ounce: A unit of weight used to measure yarn, equal to 28.5 grams.

pattern: The directions for knitting a garment. Can also refer to a stitch pattern, a group of stitches, such as "knit 1, yarnover, knit 1," knitted to create a certain design in your work.

pattern repeat: The stitches and rows that repeat to form a stitch pattern.

purl stitch: A basic stitch that looks like small chains when knitted across a row.

raglan: The armhole and sleeve shaping of a sweater that slants from the edge of the neck to the armhole.

ribbing: A combination of knit and purl stitches (such as "knit 2, purl 2") used to create vertical lines in a work. Ribbing is very elastic, so it's often used for cuffs, waistbands, hats, and any garment that needs to fit snugly in some place.

right side: The side of the work (usually the knitted side) that is meant to be shown when worn or used.

schematic: A line drawing of a garment with various measurements included with a pattern to help a knitter ensure an accurate fit.

seaming: Sewing two pieces of a knitted work together.

seed stitch: A stitch pattern created by knitting a "knit 1, purl 1" sequence over an odd number of stitches on both sides of your knitting. Seed stitch results in a dotted effect on both sides of your knitting.

selvedge: An edge of your knitted piece, knitted with an extra stitch for seaming. The pieces will join seamlessly.

set-in sleeve: Shaping that results in a curved effect in both the armhole and sleeve.

shaping: Increasing or decreasing the number of stitches in a piece to create a desired shape.

slip stitch: Moving a stitch from the left needle to the right without "working" it.

skein: A length of yarn wound loosely and coiled together.

sportweight: A category of thin yarn.

stash: The surplus of yarn that a knitter inevitably accumulates.

stitch: A unit of knitting. Stitches are worked horizontally and connect with each other to form rows.

stitch holder: Used for holding stitches temporarily, a stitch holder resembles a giant safety pin.

stitch marker: (also called ring marker) A small ring slipped onto a needle or stitch to mark a particular position in your knitting, such as the center of the work or on each side of a cable pattern. Stitch markers are usually made from plastic.

stockinette stitch: The most popular stitch pattern, stockinette stitch is created by knitting on the right side rows and purling on the wrong side rows, or, if knitting in the round, knitting every round (since you are only knitting the right side).

straight needles: Needles with a pointed end for working stitches and a closed end to prevent them from coming off the needle. Straight needles are a basic tool for any knitter.

super bulky, or super chunky: A category of very thick yarn.

superfine, fingering, or baby weight: A category of very thin yarn.

swift: A reel on which yarn is placed and then wound into a cylinder for ease during knitting.

three-needle bind-off: A method used to join two pieces together as the stitches are bound off.

weaving in: Weaving loose yarn tails on the wrong side of work, either through stitches or along a seam to secure the yarn.

whipstitch: A method of sewing two items together. Also known as overcast seam.

worsted: A category of medium-weight yarn.

wrong side: The side of the work (often the purled side) that is not meant to be shown when worn or used.

yard: A unit of length used to measure yarn, equal to .9144 meters or 3 feet.

yarnover: A method of increasing the number of stitches in a row by laying the working yarn over the needle before knitting or purling, thereby adding an extra stitch.

Yarn Suppliers

These are the yarn suppliers for the projects in this book. If you want to substitute a different yarn, weight and yardage guidelines are provided. Just make sure to check your gauge!

Berroco, Inc.
14 Elmdale Rd.
PO Box 367
Uxbridge, MA 01569
(508) 278-2527
info@berroco.com
www.berroco.com

Brown Sheep Co., Inc.
100662 County Rd. 16
Mitchell, NE 69357
(308) 635-2198
www.brownsheep.com

Cascade Yarns, Inc.
PO Box 58168
1224 Andover Park East
Tukwila, WA 98188
(206) 574-0440
www.cascadeyarns.com

Classic Elite Yarns
122 Western Ave.
Lowell, MA 01851-1434
(978) 453-2837
www.classiceliteyarns.com

Colinette Yarns
Distributed in the United States
    by Unique Kolours
28 N. Bacton Hill Rd.
Malvern, PA 19355
(610) 644-4885
www.uniquekolours.com
www.colinette.com.

JCA Crafts
35 Scales Ln.
Townsend, MA 01469-1094
(978) 597-8794
customerservice@jcacrafts.com
www.jcacrafts.com

Koigu Wool Designs
RR# 1
Williamsford, ON ,
    Canada N0H 2V0
(519) 794-3066
info@koigu.com
www.koigu.com

Lana Grossa
Distributed in the United States
    and Canada by Unicorn
    Books & Crafts, Inc.
1338 Ross St.
Petaluma, CA 94954
(707) 762-3362
unicorn@unicornbooks.com
lanagrossa.com

Louet Sales
808 Commerce Park Dr.
Odgensburg, NY 13669
(613) 925-4502
info@louet.com
www.louet.com

Muench Yarns
1323 Scott St.
Petaluma, CA 94954-1135
(707) 763-9377
info@muenchyarns.com
www.muenchyarns.com

Manos del Uruguay
Distributed in the United States
    by Design Source
PO Box 770
Medford, MA 02155
(888) 566-9970

**Plymouth Yarn
    Company**
PO Box 28
Bristol, PA 19007
(215) 788-0459
pyc@plymouthyarn.com
www.plymouthyarn.com

Rowan Yarns
Distributed in the United States
    by Westminster Fibers
4 Townsend West, Unit 8
Nashua, NH 03063
(603) 886-5041
info@westminsterfibers.com
www.knitrowan.com.

Tahki/Stacy Charles
70–30 80th St., Bldg 36
Ridgewood, NY 11385
(800) 338-YARN
www.tahkistacycharles.com

Resources

Supplies

While you may have fabulous knitting and craft stores in your neighborhood, here are a few more places you can pick up materials.

Eucalan
Find out where to purchase this gentle wool wash, perfect for washing your handknitted garments. info@eucalan.com; www.eucalan.com; (800) 561-9731.

Patternworks
This comprehensive website and catalog features many yarn brands and supplies for knitters. PO Box 1618, Center Harbor, NH 03226; (800) 723-9210; customerservice@patternworks.com; www.patternworks.com.

Rosie's Yarn Cellar
The website for this Philadelphia yarn shop is well organized and stocked with the latest and most popular yarns. The patterns in this book were designed by Rosie's owner and staff. 2017 Locust St., Philadelphia, PA 19103; (215) 977-9276; www.rosiesyarncellar.com.

Hilltop Yarn and Needlepoint Shop
The Seattle yarn shop is chockablock full of yummy yarns and materials. The website allows you to order staff-designed patterns and sign up for classes.
2224 Queen Anne Ave. North, Seattle, WA 98109; (206) 282-1332;
Hilltop Yarn East, 10635 NE 8th St., Ste. 104, Bellevue, WA 98004; (425) 452-1248;
www.hilltopyarn.com.

Books

These titles are perfect for new knitters and feature some creative and manageable projects.

Foster, Viv, ed. *Knitting Handbook*. San Diego, California: Thunder Bay Press, 2004.
Myers, Lisa R. *The Joy of Knitting*. Philadelphia: Running Press Book Publishers, 2001.
————*The Joy of Knitting Companion*. Philadelphia: Running Press Book Publishers, 2003.
Percival, Kris. *Knitting Pretty: Simple Instructions for 30 Fabulous Projects*. San Francisco: Chronicle Books, 2002.

Square, Vicki. *The Knitter's Companion*. Loveland, Colorado: Interweave Press, 1996.

Stoller, Debbie. *Stitch 'n Bitch: The Knitter's Handbook*. New York: Workman
Publishing, 2003.

Swartz, Judith L. *Hip to Knit: 18 Contemporary Projects for Today's Knitter*. Loveland,
Colorado: Interweave Press, 2002.

Thomas, Nancy J. *Knitting and Crocheting*. New York: Barnes & Noble Books, 2004.

Magazines

Interweave Knits: Quarterly magazine published by Interweave Press, Loveland,
Colorado; www.interweave.com.

Rowan Knitting Magazine: Published twice a year by Rowan Yarns, Holmfirth, England;
www.knitrowan.com.

Knitter's: Published quarterly by XRX, Inc., Sioux Falls, South Dakota;
www.knittersuniverse.com.

Vogue Knitting International: Published three times a year by Soho Publishing
Company, New York; www.vogueknitting.com.

Websites

There are loads of fabulous websites waiting to instruct you and inspire you.
A couple of favorites:

www.interweave.com: Learn about all sorts of crafts from needlework to beading and check out fun, free patterns and articles.

www.knittinguniverse.com: Find out about upcoming knitting events in your area and even learn to knit with the site's "video knit retro school" feature.

Index